For Kristan and Thomas

Zero Tolerance Policing:
Edited by Roger Hopkins Burke

ZERO TOLERANCE POLICING

Edited by

Roger Hopkins Burke

Perpetuity Press

Published by Perpetuity Press Ltd
PO Box 376 Leicester LE2 3ZZ
Telephone: +44 (0) 116 270 4186
Fax: +44 (0) 116 270 7742
Email: info@perpetuitypress.co.uk
Website: http://www.perpetuitypress.co.uk/securitybooks/

British Library Cataloguing in Publication Data.
A catalogue record for this book is available from the British Library.

ISBN 1 899287 52 3

Printed and bound in Great Britain by
Biddles Ltd, Guildford and King's Lynn

Perpetuity Press

Contents

Acknowledgements

I would like to offer my sincerest thanks to the following: my colleagues at the Scarman Centre for the Study of Public Order, Martin Gill, Adam Edwards, Ken Livingstone and Mike Rowe for reading and discussing various drafts; the staff at Perpetuity Press for their help and assistance; the copy editor, Neil Christie, for his invaluable advice; and, most importantly, the authors who have made this collection possible.

Roger Hopkins Burke
Scarman Centre
University of Leicester
March, 1998

Chapter 1

Introducing Zero Tolerance

Roger Hopkins Burke

> In all five police departments I've headed, I have followed George Kelling's prime directive: reduce disorder and you WILL (emphasis in original) reduce crime. The strategy is sending a strong message to those who commit minor crimes that they will be held responsible for their acts. The message goes like this: behave in public spaces, or the police will take action. Police will also check you out to make sure that you are not creating chronic problems or wanted for some other more serious offense. Police also will question you about what you know about other neighborhood crime.
>
> Former New York City Police Commissioner William Bratton[1]

'Zero tolerance' policing has received considerable attention from both politicians and the media both in the USA and the UK during the past three years. There are variations in definition and implementation but, in general, zero tolerance is an inclusive term for a series of policing strategies theoretically informed by the 'broken windows' philosophy. This proposes that unrepaired vandalised property and incivilities on the streets in a neighbourhood send out a message that nobody cares and produce an atmosphere in which serious crime will flourish.[2] Adapted by the proponents of 'zero tolerance'-style policing strategies – see the quotation at the top of this page – it is proposed that the police can arrest a tendency towards serious criminal behaviour in a neighbourhood by proactively and assertively confronting anti-social behaviour, minor offenders and 'quality of life' offences.[3]

Supporters of zero tolerance-style policing point to large reductions in the recorded crime figures as incontestable evidence of its success.[4] Opponents observe the failure to establish a causal link between implementation and outcomes and, perhaps more damagingly, identify an illiberal backlash directed against the excluded and oppressed with a prediction of, at best, the further alienation of local populations in 'high-risk' neighbourhoods and, at worst, widespread social disorder.[5] The positions of supporters and opponents seem incompatible.

This book provides a forum for informed debate between academics and practitioners with a range of professional interests and viewpoints on the issue of zero tolerance-style policing. The collection is published in the spirit of what might be considered 'new times', in the aftermath of the election of a government in the UK that has promised a 'new politics' beyond doctrinal dogma and that seems prepared to consider policy options from a wide range of perspectives.[6] From this standpoint there is a recognition that good ideas – and for that matter, bad ones – are not the sole preserve of one side of the traditional left/ right political dichotomy. They can emerge from many different sources and there can be a diverse range of motivations for implementing a policy or strategy.[7]

It is in the context of this new post-ideological political climate that this book provides a platform for both supporters and critics of zero tolerance. The objective is to examine both the differences and the commonalties between their various viewpoints and seek the possibility of an agreed basis for the adoption of this style of policing.

It is my purpose in the first contribution to this volume – 'A Contextualisation of Zero Tolerance Policing Strategies' – to critically examine the necessary socio-cultural pre-conditions for the successful implementation of widely acceptable zero tolerance-style policing strategies. First, the arguments of proponents and opponents of zero tolerance policing are examined and located in the context of discourses on contemporary policing approaches. Second, there is a critical examination of the socio-political context in which these strategies were introduced and have been sustained in the high-profile context of New York City. Third, the transferability of this style of policing to the UK is considered through an examination of the contemporary socio-cultural context in which crime takes place in that society.

The third chapter – 'A Question of Confidence: Zero Tolerance and Problem-Oriented Policing' – is written by Chief Superintendent Terry Romeanes who is the senior police officer responsible for the high-profile introduction of recent policing initiatives in Cleveland in the UK. The paper challenges the widely-held view that 'zero tolerance' and 'problem-oriented policing' are incompatible policing philosophies.[8] There is a consideration of the different contemporary styles of policing in existence in Cleveland, the compatibility of these is explored, and some of the early successes achieved with these methods are outlined and discussed.

The fourth chapter – 'Zero Tolerance Policing: Striking the Balance, Rights and Liberties' – is written by John Wadham, the Director of Liberty (formerly the National Council for Civil Liberties). It is the purpose of this paper to warn us of the potential civil liberties implications of zero tolerance-style policing and to alert us to the issue of police accountability for their actions.

The fifth chapter – 'Below Zero Tolerance: The New York Experience' – is written by Professor Eli Silverman from John Jay College of Criminal Justice who has been responsible for an extensive research project investigating the zero tolerance-style policing initiative introduced in New York City. It is the purpose of this paper to challenge some commonly held fallacies promoted by critics of that initiative. The view that zero tolerance-style policing strategies are contrary to the concept of policing by consent is challenged and countered.

The sixth chapter – 'Policing The Excluded Society' – is written from the academic perspective of Dr Chris Crowther, who observes that the notion of 'zero tolerance' policing has had a profound impact on recent political and public debate about social exclusion, crime and disorder. The paper examines different ideas about zero tolerance policing in the context of a wider discussion of contemporary policing styles, and there is a particular focus on the contention that the bulk of police work has throughout history targeted excluded groups in society. In this context there is a discussion of the view that zero tolerance-style policing strategies are primarily directed against the so-called 'underclass' which is made up of excluded groups such as the homeless and beggars and/or the 'rough working class'.

The seventh chapter – 'Begging, Vagrancy and Disorder' – also considers the policing of excluded groups in society. This paper addresses a conundrum that raises significant issues for zero tolerance-style policing strategies. On the one hand, beggars and vagrants can be considered an excluded class worthy of humanitarian consideration; on the other hand, large numbers of these people provide an often intimidating presence to be negotiated by ordinary people going about their legitimate activities. The concept of begging and vagrancy is both located in a historical context and considered in the context of the contemporary UK.

The final chapter – 'The 'Slide to Ashes': An Antidote to Zero Tolerance' – is written by a community policing practitioner, Bob Knights. The paper proposes that 'zero tolerance'-style policing is based on an inappropriate reading of the 'broken windows' thesis[9] and presents an alternative model which, it is argued, provides a more accurate reflection of that philosophy. It is also argued that while successful crime prevention strategies should be sustainable, long-term and cost-effective, certain applications of zero tolerance are labour-intensive and/or short term. A model is introduced – the 'slide to ashes' – devised as a means of predicting and preventing crime and disorder in educational premises but, it is proposed, with wider potential applications in society. It is suggested that the more subliminal ethos of the 'slide' is more sustainable, cost-effective and more easily adopted and incorporated into management practices than the short-term solution of zero tolerance-style policing.

Finally, the concluding comments summarise the various contributions to this volume and locate them in the context of an argument that proposes that proactive, confident, assertive, policing strategies could be part of a general and widely accepted quality of life initiative in society.

Notes

1 Quoted on the cover of Kelling, G.L. and Coles, C.M. (1996) *Fixing Broken Windows: Restoring Order and Reducing Crime in Our Communities*. New York: The Free Press.

2 Wilson, J.Q. and Kelling, G.L. (1982) Broken Windows. *Atlantic Monthly*, March, 1982, pp 29-38.

3 Obviously, not all minor offenders are involved in serious offences. They can, however, be an excellent source of intelligence.

4   Bratton, W.J. (1997) Crime is Down in New York City: Blame the Police. In Dennis, N. (ed.) *Zero Tolerance: Policing a Free Society*. London: Institute for Economic Affairs; Dennis, N. and Mallon, R. (1997) Confident Policing in Hartlepool. In Dennis, N. (ed.), op cit.

5   See Morgan, R. (1997) Swept Along by Zero Option. *The Guardian*, 22 January; Read, S. (1997) Below Zero. *Police Review*, 17 January; Pollard, C. (1997) Zero-Tolerance: Short-Term Fix, Long-Term Liability. In Dennis, N. (ed.), op cit.; Crowther, C. (1998) 'Policing The Excluded Society' in this volume.

6   The Prime Minister, Tony Blair, and his Home Secretary, Jack Straw, have both made highly publicised statements supportive of 'zero tolerance' policing. See Travis, A. (1996) Atlantic Cuffings. *The Guardian*, 21 November; Blair, T. (1997) Interview with Tony Blair. *The Big Issue*, 8 January.

7   See Giddens, A. (1994) *Beyond Left and Right*. Cambridge: Polity.

8   Morgan, R. (1997) op cit; Read, S. (1997) op cit; Pollard, C. (1997) op cit.

9   Wilson, J.Q. and Kelling, G.L. (1982) op cit.

Chapter 2

A Contextualisation of Zero Tolerance Policing Strategies

Roger Hopkins Burke

Introduction

It was noted in the introduction to this volume that while proponents of 'zero tolerance'-style policing point to large reductions in the recorded crime figures as evidence of its success, their opponents both dispute the existence of a causal link between implementation and outcomes while noting a 'high-risk' potential for serious public disorder. There appears to be no basis for compromise between two apparently incompatible positions.

It is the purpose of this paper to critically examine the socio-cultural preconditions that would be necessary for the successful implementation of a form of zero tolerance-style policing that might prove acceptable to a very wide range of public opinion. The structure is as follows. First, the arguments of proponents and opponents of zero tolerance policing are explored and located both in the context of the theoretical foundations of the concept and in terms of discourses on contemporary policing styles. Second, there is a critical examination of the socio-political context in which this style of policing was first introduced and has subsequently been sustained in New York City. The discussion includes an exploration of the nature of contemporary post-industrial – or postmodern – communities and the distinct problems these pose for those charged with responsibility for governing and policing them. Third, there is a consideration of the necessary preconditions for the successful implementation of zero tolerance-style policing strategies in the UK.[1] This discussion includes an examination of the socio-cultural context of that society and the forms of crime and criminal behaviour that provide a challenge for the contemporary police service.

The core argument of this paper is founded on three propositions. First, it is proposed that there is a general consumer demand in society – and that this exists among all ethnic and other interest groups – for a highly visible police presence on the streets. Second, the nature of that presence must be sensitive to the policing requirements of the particular community in order to gain widespread support and legitimacy. Third, the policing strategies employed can be proactive, confident and assertive as long as they are perceived as 'fair' by the local community.

We will start with an examination of the theoretical foundations of zero tolerance-style policing, a presentation of the basic arguments of its proponents and opponents and a discussion of recent styles of policing.

Zero tolerance policing: proponents and opponents

We should note at the outset that 'zero tolerance' is a soundbite[2] term regularly used by the media and politicians but virtually never employed by senior police officers or its academic supporters. It is a generic expression used to describe a variety of – what I here refer to as – proactive, confident, assertive policing strategies. There are variations in these strategies but, in general, they are theoretically informed by the 'broken windows' thesis, developed in the USA in the early 1980s by two criminologists, James Q. Wilson and George Kelling.[3] In short, this thesis asserts that just as an unrepaired broken window is a sign that nobody cares and leads to more damage, minor incivilities – such as begging, public drunkenness, vandalism and graffiti – if unchecked and uncontrolled, produce an atmosphere in a community in which more serious crime will flourish. Over time, individuals may feel that they can get away with minor offences, which leads them to commit more serious offences.

Proponents of zero tolerance-style policing, for example William J. Bratton the former Commissioner of Police for New York City,[4] and Superintendent Ray Mallon of the Cleveland Constabulary in the UK,[5] have adapted the 'broken windows' thesis to argue that a positive police presence targeting petty offenders on the streets can lead to substantial reductions in the level of crime and they point to the success of experiments in their own constituencies to support these assertions. During the period 1994 to 1996 the official statistics[6] purport to show the crime rate in New York City to have decreased by 37% – the homicide rate alone by 50%[7] – and in Hartlepool, Cleveland, the total of reported crimes was reduced by 27% during the same period.[8]

Opponents of zero tolerance-style policing strategies observe not only a lack evidence supporting a direct causal link between these initiatives and any apparent decline in the crime figures, but they also consider these tactics a return to the failed military-style policing tactics pursued by metropolitan forces in inner-city neighbourhoods in the UK during the 1970s and early 1980s. 'Swamp 81' is invariably cited as being highly indicative of that style of policing: a proactive police operation conducted in South-West London designed to detect street robbers or 'muggers', it resulted in over 1,000 predominantly black youths being stopped and searched, of whom fewer than 100 were charged with criminal offences.[9] The inquiry report into the subsequent riot suggested that the style of policing had contributed substantially to the disorder.[10]

Commentators on both the left and right of the political spectrum – and on both sides of the Atlantic – are in agreement in criticising military-style policing. The American political scientist James Q. Wilson – associated with the political right and the co-author of the 'broken windows' thesis[11] – has argued that increased police activity targeted at 'crime areas' can appear racist because black people make up a large proportion of the low-class crime-prone populations.[12] Furthermore, actual police racism leads to mistrust of the service by those they purport to serve. The consequence of this racism – both actual and perceived – is that the information flow on which the police depend in order to successfully do their jobs ceases and they subsequently come to feel that the local population holds them in contempt.

The British criminologists John Lea and Jock Young – from the perspective of their new 'left realism', which has subsequently become very influential with the current Labour Government – specifically criticised 'Swamp 81'.[13] They argue that reductions in crime that apparently occur as a result of assertive policing may actually result from a consequent unwillingness to report crime by an oppressed public. This policing amounts to the brutalisation of the neighbourhood, which in turn leads to more, not less, crime by the inhabitants. Furthermore, illegal actions – perceived or actual – committed by over-enthusiastic officers provoke younger inhabitants by bringing home to them their own powerlessness. Apparent unfairness and racism reduce the flow of information from the public, which in turn forces the police to become still more oppressive in order to achieve their ends of arresting offenders. Losing the support of the local community forces officers to rely heavily on stereotypes. This increases the impression of unfairness, and the vicious circle is complete.

Lea and Young observe the outcome of military-style policing strategies to be that the police come to be considered the enemy of the community and offenders are secretly or even overtly admired and given sanctuary. They note that the police in Brixton consequently resorted to the use of random stop and search powers both as a substitute for receiving information from the public and as a form of generalised deterrence. It was said in evidence to the subsequent Scarman inquiry that:

> even if police officers behaved with impeccable courtesy towards every person stopped
> and searched and apologised to those found not to be carrying suspect items, many
> people would resent being treated as suspects when innocently walking to the tube
> or home.[14]

In summary, the argument against military-style policing, stereotypical suspect identification and indiscriminate searching of citizens extends beyond allegations of alleged 'unfairness'. Such strategies are actually counter-productive: they actually lessen the quality of information flowing to the police which is vital in detecting serious offenders. They also act as an extension of the labelling process: by labelling entire communities 'criminal', the police themselves attract the label 'enemy' Not only do they learn less than they otherwise would about instrumental offences, but they also tend to provoke public order offences such as occurred in Brixton during April 1981.

The Scarman Report[15] into those disorders stressed that all aspects of police work should be premised upon *active community consent, trust* and *participation*. Society needed to recognise that the police working on their own could not make a significant impact on local crime problems. Effective crime prevention was the responsibility of the whole community.[16] Consequently, during the course of the 1980s, the public police service underwent a process of moving towards 'community policing' by adjusting to take account of local people's perceptions, priorities and expectations. They began to develop proactive styles and strategies which were sensitive to the needs of different audiences with the intention of breaking the cycle of antagonism and alienation that existed between the police and some local communities.[17] Community policing was to become the orthodoxy in the UK.

There is, however, no universally accepted definition of community policing. In its simplest form it is described as returning as many officers as possible to foot patrol duties. At the other end of the scale, it involves establishing systems to implement procedures whereby the local community and various agencies may participate in the decision-making, style and level of policing most beneficial to that community.[18] It will be helpful to examine the concept more closely.

David Smith usefully identifies three broad themes concerning the idea of community in social policy.[19] First, there is a reaction against the large scale and remoteness which is associated with a demand for decentralisation, consultation and participation in decision-making by local communities. Second, there is a suggestion that people should come together to meet their common needs and tackle problems; and third, there is an understanding that public policy and practice should act to strengthen voluntary and informal structures and work with, not against, them. Smith observes that these ideas have been expressed in the field of policing policy and practice in six closely-linked ways in the UK.

First, great emphasis is placed upon the importance of permanent beat officers who patrol small areas and get to know the local people and their problems. Second, a greater prominence is given to prevention (proactive strategies) than apprehension (reactive strategies), with a co-ordinated approach to the development and implementation of these tactics advocated. Third, there is the promotion of a multi-agency approach to problem-solving. Fourth, improved consultation combined with decentralisation and devolution of power has been proposed. The introduction of consultative groups and lay visits to police stations are identified as important initiatives in this respect. Fifth, a greater prominence is given to activities initiated by the police rather than responding to calls for service from the public. Sixth, a much greater emphasis is placed on the importance of informal social controls as it is argued that the police can do little or nothing on their own and that they need the help and support of their communities to carry out their roles effectively.

In practice, this particular conceptualisation of community policing, which tends to be the favoured model of opponents of assertive zero tolerance-style policing, has not produced the intended outcomes. Smith identifies the following reasons for this failure. First, beat officers have been far from permanent, they have often been required to perform other duties and have been unable to get to know their public. Consequently, there has been no improvement in the visibility of the police to local people and at the same time there has been no decrease in the levels of crime. Second, while there has been some progress in developing a co-ordinated approach to problem-solving there has been a reluctance on the part of some agencies to become involved with the police, and for many of those that have, such initiatives were not placed sufficiently high on their agenda. Finally, police consultative groups have not achieved the objectives for which they were established.[20] True consultation was not taking place because members were not able to engage in discussions on an equal footing with police managers as they did not have sufficient information or the necessary professional advice or expertise. In short, community policing strategies starved of resources and commitment from senior police and other agency management were plainly failing to reduce crime or satisfy the demands of the public. In the face of ever-increasing crime figures community policing was perceived not to be working.[21]

For the purist proponent of this apparently failed community policing model the problem has been inadequate implementation. The introduction of assertive zero tolerance policing strategies is simply a backward step to the deeply flawed military-style policies of the 1970s and early 1980s and they carry the same inherent risk of widespread public disorder.[22] From this point of view, it is preferable that the police have a tolerant attitude to minor criminal activity among such groups in order to avoid further alienation and potential serious social unrest.[23] It is a perspective that nonetheless appears to lack support among widespread sections of the public. *Ignore BWT!*

Crime surveys repeatedly show that the public continue to want a visible police presence on the streets.[24] Senior police officers and their academic supporters, however, presumably ever-mindful of the failure of the community policing philosophy to deliver tangible results, have argued that there are insufficient available resources for such a strategy[25] and that those police professionals who promise the public otherwise are guilty of 'dishonest policing.'[26] Now it is possible to observe here an extremely convenient convergence between two discourses – on the one hand, a liberal/libertarian criminal justice perspective that proposes that the police should withdraw from whole areas of the social world in order that they do not further criminalise groups of dispossessed unfortunates, and, on the other hand, the material concerns of senior police management who have the problem of managing limited resources. There appears a most convenient justification for doing little.

For some years this considered withdrawal from the streets, dressed up in liberal guise, was *de facto* policing policy in both the USA and the UK.[27] In general, it had gone unchallenged until the introduction in the USA of a different style – from the UK model – of community policing where the police take the lead with the introduction of proactive, *def.* confident, assertive policing strategies that have come to be termed zero tolerance.[28] Friedmann provides us with a basis for theorising this more assertive conceptualisation of community policing. He begins by proposing that we examine the notion from three different perspectives.[29]

positive

First, from the point of view of the police, there is the need to improve ties with the community in order to gain assistance in the fight against crime. There is a need to increase levels of perceived legitimacy for police tactics and actions in order to improve the flow of intelligence from the public. Second, from the perspective of the community, there is a growing recognition of the need for improved police services while at the same time having a greater say in how policing decisions are made. Third, from the point of view of both the community *and* the police, it is argued that: a) the police on their own can have little control over crime and other acts of antisocial behaviour; b) crime control needs to focus on those factors that cause or provide the opportunity for crime or antisocial behaviour to occur; c) proactive policing strategies should be the norm, replacing in some instances reactive policing; d) decentralised community-oriented policing is a prerequisite to the introduction of this type of initiative; e) a greater focus should be placed on targeting 'quality of life' issues; and f) greater consideration should be given to individual civil rights and liberties. Friedmann consolidates these issues in terms of the following definition:

> Community policing is a policy and a strategy aimed at achieving more effective and efficient crime control, reduced fear of crime, improved quality of life, im- proved police services and police legitimacy, through a pro-active reliance on com- munity resources that seeks to change crime causing conditions. It assumes a need for greater accountability of police, greater public share in decision-making and greater concerns for civil rights and liberties.[30]

It will be shown in this paper that those zero tolerance-style policing strategies that aspire to widespread legitimacy and success are clearly compatible with this definition. In short, they are part of a revised form of community policing in which the police service takes a proactive, confident and assertive *lead* in seeking to confront and control crime but which at the same time is highly dependent upon the support of the community it purports to serve.

The argument presented in this section can be summarised as follows. Proponents of zero tolerance-style policing argue that a positive police presence targeting petty offenders on the streets can lead to substantial reductions in the level of crime. Opponents note an absence of objective evidence to establish a direct causal link between these initiatives and the apparent decline in the crime figures. More damagingly, they consider these tactics a return to the failed military-style policing tactics abandoned in the aftermath of the inner-city riots that occurred in the UK during the early 1980s. They propose a more effective implementation of the community style of policing introduced in the UK at that time. On the other hand, zero tolerance-style policing can be conceptualised as part of a revised form of community policing, with its origins in the USA, where the police overcome the apparent weaknesses of the failed earlier model by taking a proactive lead in confronting crime.

It was in New York City that a highly publicised policing initiative – implicitly founded on this later conceptualisation of community policing and later termed zero tolerance by politicians and the world media – was introduced. The following three sections of the paper provide a critical examination of the socio-political context in which this style of policing was first introduced and has subsequently been sustained in New York City. The following section will commence by sharing some observations about my own personal experiences that were significant in shaping the thinking that underpins this paper.

New York City – a personal awakening

In June 1995 I visited New York City. Shortly after arrival I narrowly avoided being knocked down by the perpetrator of a traffic violation and during the next three weeks repeatedly observed similar incidents. What really surprised me, however, was the large numbers of police officers standing around on the street corners of Midtown Manhattan seemingly ignoring these misdemeanours. I later mentioned this to some senior officers, and the collective polite but world-weary response can be summarised by the following comment (delivered with an appropriate shrug):

> Look, this is New York City. Cops aren't paid very much – they just want to get in their 20 years (before retirement). Who needs some crazy guy blowing your head off?

The implication was clear – being a police officer in New York City was perceived as a dangerous occupation and a key motivation was to stay alive.[31] Dealing with minor transgressions apparently carried a high risk.[32] Now this was a significant admission. People involved in minor violations of the criminal code were likely to be involved in other more serious criminal activities. It was – as we have seen above – an increasing recognition of this situation that had provided the preconditions for the community policing revolution that was to become known as zero tolerance. The socio-political conditions in which that policing revolution was instigated and became widely acceptable to the public in New York City are highly significant.

During the course of my three-week stay in New York City, Police Commissioner Bill Bratton and his boss Mayor Rudolph Giuliani were constantly featured on the local television news programme.[33] The latter was the first Republican Mayor for over sixty years. Previously a district attorney, he had been elected the previous year after campaigning on the issue of crime and disorder – specifically on the issue of dealing with aggressive 'squeegee men'.[34] He had subsequently appointed Bratton to develop initiatives to deal with the crime problems and had then himself co-ordinated the activities of other city agencies to support these strategies.[35]

At first sight, Giuliani is a straightforward right-wing Republican with an agenda based on a marriage of authoritarian social policies and free market economics epitomised by his welfare budget-slashing policies and his 'get tough' approach to policing.[36] Indeed, Bratton firmly locates this policing revolution in terms of a reaction to the post-Vietnam liberal/libertarian discourse that had come to dominate US public life.[37] Closer examination, however, reveals a more complex picture.

New York City is an intensely populated metropolis of fragmented and diverse communities that could best be described as – to use the language of contemporary social science – postmodern in nature. The evidence examined below suggests that Mayor Giuliani can be conceptualised as a new-style – postmodern – politician who is alert to at least some of the implications of trying to govern such a society. However, before discussing that contention in more detail, it is appropriate here to examine the notion of postmodernity –

and the modernity it aspires to succeed – a little more closely.

Modernity and postmodernity

The term postmodernism is appearing ever more frequently in social science texts and the first books to explore the implications for the field of criminal justice have recently appeared.[38] Unfortunately, the terminology used is invariably difficult to access. The key ideas are, however, really quite straightforward and are presented here in a concise and accessible form. I will start by defining the term *modern*.

Modern societies are mass societies: mass production and consumption, corporate capital and organised labour, an economically organising interventionist state that aspires to full employment, demand management and public investment in health, education and welfare.[39] They are essentially characterised by moral certainty and confidence in the explanatory power of grand social and political theories to solve the problems of humanity. There are competing ways of seeing and dealing with the world – for example, liberalism, conservatism, socialism – but the devotees of these various perspectives believe in the fundamental capacity of *their* doctrine to solve all problems in society.

These grand theories or *metanarratives* are usually presented as representing the perceived material interests of mass groups or social classes – the bourgeoisie, the middle and the working classes – often portrayed as a struggle between the interests of capital and labour. Consequently, modern societies are characterised by political parties of the left and right who each purport to have *the* solution to *all* the problems of that society. They have striven to develop programmes that satisfy the different class interests of the mass of society – in the main, through the facilitation of economic conditions to enhance the reproduction of capitalist development while at the same time providing 'cradle to grave' welfare provisions for the workers – and are relatively successful because modern societies tend to share core social values.

There has been a considerable debate among scholars as to how that social consensus has developed and been maintained. The role of the church, education system, and mass media have all been cited at various times as helping to inculcate a dominant ideology into the minds of the modern citizenry.[40] Others have pointed to the role of the public police service in targeting non-respectable elements of the working classes and other potentially subversive groups in the pursuit of these goals.[41]

In recent years there have been ever increasing doubts about the sustainability of the modernist project in an increasingly fragmented and diverse social world that some social scientists refer to as the postmodern condition.[42] Economically, this involves the rejection of mass production-line technology in favour of flexible working patterns and a flexible labour force with a greater stress on enterprise and entrepreneurialism.[43] Politically, the traditional parties of the 'left' and 'right' have proved inadequate to the task of representing myriad interest groups as diverse as major industrialists and financiers, small business proprietors, the unemployed and dispossessed, wide-ranging gender and sexual preference interests, environmentalists, the homeless and the socially excluded.[44]

Postmodern politics are consequently complex and characterised by moral ambiguity, with the recognition of a range of different discourses that can be legitimate and hence right for different people, at different times, in different contexts. It is a perspective founded on cultural relativism, the notion that there are a series of legitimate discourses on a particular issue and that it is difficult, if not impossible, to objectively choose between them. The objective truth – or competing objective realities – of modernity, are replaced by a recognition of the multiple realities or moral ambiguities of postmodernity.

It is a situation that raises all kinds of difficulties for politicians and political parties because few of these varied views and discourses sit easily and exclusively within the traditional boundaries of left/right modernist political thinking. The successful postmodern politician, therefore, has to balance these ambiguities in order to gain a coalition of support. Indeed, they will probably have to build a whole range of coalitions across a whole range of issues.

Having examined these notions of modern and postmodern society in the abstract, we now explore the practical implications of these observations for New York City.

Postmodernity and New York City

New York City is undoubtedly a postmodern metropolis characterised by a mixture of diverse and fragmented communities with a wide range of interests and concerns. Consequently, the aspiring successful politician has to be aware of the need to build coalitions between these diverse groups. The following example serves to illustrate this point.

During my June 1995 visit, Mayor Giuliani was faced with a political conundrum. New York's large and electorally significant gay and lesbian community was preparing for its annual parade on Fifth Avenue. Giuliani had decided that he should go on the march. Unfortunately, the route involved marching past St Patrick's Cathedral, the spiritual home to the large and influential Catholic minority who are vehemently anti-gay and the target, during the previous year's parade, of insults from lesbian women exposing themselves topless. Giuliani resolved the issue by marching on the parade but by briefly leaving it while it went past the Cathedral. In postmodern political terms there appears to be a recognition of the validity of two very different discourses for their adherents and the need to strike a balance between their interests.

There is, however, little long-term future in attempting to build lasting political coalitions on such knife-edge agendas. It would certainly be impossible to build a successful coalition on all issues. The aspiring electorally successful postmodern politician therefore needs to identify crucial political issues that concern the widest possible range of interest groups. The issue identified by Giuliani was that of crime. New York City was widely recognised as the crime capital of the world, its people were scared and they wanted something doing about the problem.[45] Mayor Giuliani was elected to office determined to do something about the issue.[46]

It was in this socio-political context that Giuliani – supporting his determination with a willingness to provide funds for additional officers, initiatives and equipment[47] – appointed William J. Bratton Police Commissioner with a mandate to target crime. Bratton enacted this mandate by introducing a computerised managerial system known as 'CompStat' into the NYPD.[48] The present Commissioner Howard Safir describes this as:

> A crime management tool which uses weekly crime statistics, computer mapping and intensive strategy sessions to direct the implementation of crime fighting strategies.[49]

Safir claims that this management system has:

> Reorganised and refocused the NYPD on its fundamental mission of fighting and preventing crime and disorder. It's given the department the tactical flexibility to track and hit the moving target of crime. It's given us the capability to manage crime instead of letting crime manage us.[50]

CompStat operates by the police commanders for each borough giving periodical briefings to the senior management of the NYPD. These take place in the central command room of the Department which is set out like a wartime operations centre. The management team sit around a horseshoe-shaped desk while the borough commander stands in the middle. The crime statistics for the borough are displayed on screens behind the commander whether they want them there or not. What statistics are displayed are selected by the management team as the commander gives the briefing. There is one CompStat meeting a week and the borough commanders do not know which of them are going to be called to give a briefing. Each commander has therefore to prepare a briefing each week on the chance that they may have to give a presentation.

There can be little doubt that these often 'brutal' periodical interrogations of borough commanders by NYPD senior management in an environment that resembles a wartime operations centre have provided sufficient motivation to achieve success in the fight against crime.[51] It is a management system that has been most noticeably used to target 'quality of life' crimes – the so-called 'zero tolerance' policing strategy – as a means of recovering the streets of New York City for the law-abiding citizen.[52] Furthermore, it is a style of policing that has remained politically popular with an extremely large cross-cultural section of the population. In the next section we examine why this should be the case.

Policing the postmodern city

Professor Eli Silverman in his contribution to this volume dismisses accusations of aggression and bullying made by critics of the NYPD and asserts that 'zero tolerance' policing strategies have the widespread support of the populace. Certainly the crime figures cited in the introduction to this essay suggest a substantial reduction in the levels of recorded crime in the city and the police have undoubtedly taken the credit for this decline. Opponents of zero tolerance policing[53] – both in the USA and the UK – point to demographic factors (fewer young males in the population), the end of the crack-cocaine epidemic (undoubtedly a major reason for the explosion of crime in the United States during the late 1980s and early 1990s) and a simultaneous desire among young ghetto-raised black males to live longer and desist from shooting each other, as key factors in that crime reduction. Simple logic suggests that these factors must have been influential - indeed, it is extremely likely that they provided the sociological preconditions - but Professor Silverman has no doubt that it was the policing revolution introduced by William Bratton that was the main reason for the reduction in recorded crime.

It should be noted that Mayor Giuliani, who has taken the political credit for this phenomenon, remains extremely popular: he was re-elected in November 1997 with a greatly increased majority and electoral analysis suggests his tough stance on crime was responsible for his success.[54] There was even a 'Democrats for Giuliani' group committed to securing his re-election at a time when the Democrats were winning other elected posts in the city by large margins.[55] Seen to be successfully fighting crime seems to be an excellent means of building electoral support among the very diverse ethnic and other interest groups in New York.

Critics – as noted above – have perceived a real danger that these assertive policing tactics will be used in an insensitive fashion to target particular ethnic minority groups and that this will lead to a repeat of the inner-city unrest widespread in the UK in the early 1980s and Los Angeles in 1965 and 1992.[56] Interestingly, this has not been the case in New York City, a metropolis culturally and ethnically diverse with a large black population. We will now consider why this is so.

A good starting point is the observation by Professor Silverman – in his contribution to this volume – that the major policing demand of the black communities of New York City is for more policing. Indeed, they want the same levels of policing enjoyed by the prosperous middle-class white communities. Now this recognition should come as no surprise to those living in the UK. The lesson learned from self-report crime surveys conducted during the past 15 years is that it is the poorest sections of our societies – in particular, members of ethnic minority groups – who experience the highest level of crime victimisation in society.[57] It might therefore be reasonable to assume that ethnic minority groups have a large demand for policing. Yet, this is not the case. Many other surveys show these very same ethnic groups to be vehemently anti-police.[58] Why is this so? Because there is the widespread perception among black people – acknowledged above in the discussion of the views of right and left realist social scientists – that the police are inherently racist. They do not want police officers they consider external to their communities stopping and searching everyone they encounter simply because they are black: in other words, the kind of practice documented by the Scarman Report in the UK in its critique of military-style policing strategies.[59]

In short, a group of people substantially over-represented among crime victims – a group with a legitimate demand for quality policing, black people – have been treated 'unfairly'.

This unfairness rankles. Respectable working-class black people at a high risk of crime victimisation are discouraged from seeking help from a perceived racist police force and develop common cause with delinquent youth in their midst simply because of a shared status of being black and the victims of racism. There is a widespread demand for policing among black people, but they want fair policing. It could be argued that in some ways they currently get – and this involves a very negotiable definition – 'fairer' treatment from the NYPD than they have previously enjoyed in some parts of the UK and the USA. We will now examine that possibility a little more closely.

Life is undoubtedly hard for many people in New York City.[60] There are a great many poor people and a great percentage of these are black. There is a lot of violence, people carry guns and many still – regardless of the policing revolution that has occurred in that city during the past few years – get killed.[61] Very large numbers of black people are processed annually by the criminal justice system and many of these are incarcerated.[62] The police undoubtedly take an extremely assertive stance when dealing with many black people. Yet, I have a suspicion that the black community receives this police intervention in a more positive fashion than they did in some parts of the UK during the days of military-style policing in the 1970s and 1980s. The police may use some very 'assertive' practices, but they are perceived as being assertive with people because they are criminals and not simply because they are members of a particular ethnic group. The police are assertive but they are 'fair' and they have the respect – and this may be very grudging respect in a black community experiencing great poverty and deprivation – of the majority of law-abiding black citizens.[63] The crucial label in this context is 'criminal' rather than 'black'.

This is an extremely contentious argument. Studies have shown racism to be endemic among police officers in the USA and that black people have widely identified this as a problem.[64] Nevertheless, these issues have not been researched widely since the early to mid-1990s and the aftermath of the notorious Rodney King case in Los Angeles.[65] Times and perceptions change. Significant activity on the part of the police service has probably helped to bring about that change.

The NYPD had developed a most unenviable and widespread reputation for corruption and unprofessional behaviour.[66] It was, therefore, a central part of the Giuliani/Bratton policing revolution to both tackle that corruption and, most importantly, to be seen by the general public to be doing something. During my visit to New York City in June 1995 Commissioner Bratton was most noticeably engaged in a campaign to deal with corruption within the NYPD.[67] He had sent an unambiguous message to New Yorkers that he was going to do something significant about unprofessional behaviour within their police service. The following much publicised example provides evidence of an enduring willingness to tackle such behaviour.

Mr Louima, 30, a private security guard born in Haiti, alleged that two police officers shoved the handle of a sink plunger up his rectum and then forced it into his mouth, breaking some teeth. He also claimed that one of the officers called him a 'stupid nigger' and said, 'This is Giuliani time, not Dinkins time' – a reference to Mayor Giuliani's predecessor, who was allegedly less intolerant of criminals. Significantly, the NYPD responded swiftly. Two officers were charged with assault, the commander of the 70th Precinct and his deputy were transferred, and a desk sergeant on duty on the night of the incident was suspended. Mayor Giuliani repeatedly expressed his dismay over the incident and his sympathy for the victim. He visited Mr Louima in hospital and appeared on television to try and soothe tempers among the Haitian population. The newly installed commander of the 70th Precinct, Raymond Diaz, made a public appearance to talk to the protesters. He told *The New York Times*: 'It's understandable that they're outraged. I hope we can overcome this and get stronger'.[68] There is undoubtedly racism and other forms of unprofessional behaviour in the NYPD, but there is obviously a high-profile response on the part of the authorities both to do something about it and to be seen doing something.

The media – in particular, television – is central to the postmodern political agenda in New York City. It is the means by which politicians and public servants get across the message that they are doing something. But it is not a one-way syncopatic relationship. Public servants and politicians in New York City are constantly challenged and brought to account by television interviewers as incidents happen and develop. The public expect – and get – speedy action. Prevarication and evasiveness are not popular political strategies. The NYPD are no exceptions as the citizens of New York City are coming to expect high professional and ethical standards from their police service.

To summarise the argument so far: New York City is a diverse and fragmented society; politicians need to gain the support of diverse interest groups in order to develop a coherent programme and to stay in office; crime has been identified as an issue that can gain widespread political support and there has been a widespread consumer demand for something to be done about it; consequently, police strategies can be assertive as long as they are perceived as 'fair' and targeted against people because of what they are doing, not because of who they are; finally, this has to be seen to be the case in order for them to gain and retain the support of the communities they serve. In short, it is a contemporary form of community policing.

The question remains, however, as to whether this proactive, confident, assertive style of community policing – introduced in the postmodern context of New York City – is transferable to another locality with a different socio-cultural context, a different political agenda and tradition of policing. Such initiatives have of course also been introduced in various parts of the UK – most noticeably by Cleveland Constabulary – and that initiative is discussed by Chief Superintendent Terry Romeanes in his contribution to this volume. We will now consider the potential for this style of community policing in the context of the UK.

Crime and the postmodern condition in the contemporary UK

It is sensible that we consider the nature of a given society and pattern of crime and criminality that exists within it before considering the applicability of a particular policing strategy. It is, therefore, the purpose of this section to provide a critical examination of the socio-cultural context in which the contemporary UK police service performs its duties. During the process of establishing the nature of this context, three closely interlinked issues are of necessity examined: a) the changes in the socio-economic foundations of society that have occurred during the past 40 years; b) the ways in which the pattern of crime and criminal behaviour have apparently changed during that period; and c) explanations offered by social scientists for those changes.

In their account of working-class life in the North-East of England during the depression years of the 1930s, Professor Norman Dennis[69] and Superintendent Ray Mallon observe that although there was mass unemployment and widespread poverty there was little crime.[70] It is the crux of their argument that people were poor but basically honest. Dennis – an avid supporter of the zero tolerance-style policing strategies introduced by the Cleveland Constabulary and an influential commentator on the issue in some quarters – blames the subsequent explosion in crime on the breakdown in the respectable cultural traditions of the working class that he blames on the intellectual relativism of postmodernism.[71] The implication of his account is clear. Crime can be reduced by rebuilding the old respectable working-class cultural traditions. It is the task of the police to get out on to the streets, confront those breaking the law and, at the same time, be part of a larger project of helping to restore the moral certainties of modern society.

Clearly this would be a difficult strategy to implement. There seems little possibility of restoring the cultural contours of the past and there are probably few under the age of 40 who would wish to. The old industries – coal, steel, shipbuilding, that provided the traditional working-class solidarity and social cohesion – have largely died out in the North-East of England and, for that matter, in the rest of the UK. Recent research suggests that Indian restaurants now have a higher turnover than those previously dominant industries combined.[72] In such a changed socio-cultural environment there is likely to be little demand for the police service to be used as a blunt instrument to help restore the moral values – and the traditional social class boundaries – of a previous modernity. It is worthwhile considering that changed environment a little more closely.

Those of us born and raised in the UK are undoubtedly familiar with the apocryphal stories of how in the 'good old days' people left their doors open and neighbours entered unannounced to borrow a cup of sugar. These accounts of community and working-class solidarity are also a staple of classical sociological texts.[73] In reality, there was probably little else to borrow. The defining characteristic of the lives of the great majority of people was poverty and that was the case whether in work or not.[74] The extent of ambition for most people was to earn sufficient money to feed, clothe and keep a roof over the heads of their families. There was no television, limited radio, no videos, no motor cars for the vast majority of the population and certainly no overseas holidays. Most people were poor, had few ambitions and aspirations beyond basic survival, and in reality, many of them were rather unsophisticated. Significantly, there was a high level of social consensus and group solidarity because people had very similar life experiences.

In the language of the great French sociologist Emile Durkheim a century ago, the lives of ordinary working people – regardless of whether they lived in the great mass industrial areas or the rural countryside – were characterised by high levels of mechanical solidarity. There was a strong homogeneity of the group, likenesses and similarities between individuals and common moral sentiments binding one member to another. Severe limitations were placed on the ability of any one individual to develop a personal identity or uniqueness. Co-operation within the group was restricted to what could be achieved through the close conformity of each member to a single stereotype.[75]

Professor Geoffrey Pearson alerts us to the simplicity of this argument, warning against popularly held common-sense notions that – predominantly adolescent – criminal behaviour is a recent phenomenon; that in the past people were orderly, disciplined and well behaved.[76] He notes that concerns about young people and criminal behaviour are nothing new:

> the complaint is entirely familiar, invariably expressed in a generational time-scale which links the perceived erosion in moral standards to events of 'twenty or thirty years ago' or 'since the war'.[77]

Pearson observes that such concerns have constantly reoccurred throughout history, with a parallel assumption that things were always better in the past. Crime, of course, existed and there was drunkenness, disorder, violence, trouble at football grounds and even embryo youth subcultures.[78] But we might observe that crime was quantitatively and qualitatively different in a society characterised by poverty and very limited aspirations.[79] Poor people undoubtedly stole from each other but the level of economic gain would have been small. Theft from a neighbour would have been even less likely in the areas with the greatest group solidarity and the least money.

Norman Dennis makes much of the fact that recorded crime rates in the UK– and indeed throughout the industrialised capitalist world[80] – have soared ever upwards since 1955.[81] We should not really be surprised. Society has changed considerably in the intervening years. Wartime rationing finally ended in 1955 and the bright, brash consumer society that has produced an educated, sophisticated, affluent population of people with diverse knowledge, skills and experiences of life, was born. In the language of Emile Durkheim, the lives of people have become increasingly characterised by high levels of organic solidarity. There is less dependence on the maintenance of uniformity between individuals, and more emphasis on the management of the diverse functions of different groups. More and more scope is now given to individual conscience, aptitude and freedom of action.[82]

Perhaps the most significant development to have occurred during the intervening 40 years has been the fact that the UK has become substantially more prosperous than at any time in its history. The annual GDP figures show that the output of the economy has risen by approximately 50% since 1970 and has almost doubled since 1960.[83] But this growth in prosperity has not been equally shared. The skilled industrial worker – largely male – has disappeared, to be replaced by casualised, low-paid, temporary, part-time workers ('McJobs')[84], a growing proportion of them female.[85] Increased material affluence is often the outcome of a shift towards double-income families, where both parents work but also spend less time with their children, and lone parenthood, with its associated signifi-cant social consequences.[86] Perhaps most significantly, the qualitative experience of pov-erty and unemployment today is substantially different than in the past.

Life in the 1920s and the 1930s was characterised by a generalised, shared working- class experience of poverty, whether in work or not. Today, the level of home ownership is substantially higher than in the past, car ownership and holidays in increasingly more exotic overseas locations are becoming far more widespread. The workless and homeless live alongside, or at least not far from, the relatively affluent. The wonders and delights of the consumer society are aggressively advertised during the low-budget television pro-grammes churned out 24 hours a day to entertain the 'new leisure classes'.[87]

The contemporary economically dispossessed have very different aspirations than their predecessors 60 years ago. Many aspire to the products they see in the television com-mercials and they are not easily distracted from these ambitions. They do not accept long-term unemployment and poverty in the same stoic fashion as their predecessors vividly described in the various accounts of Norman Dennis.[88] They have legitimate aspirations to a share in the 'good life'.

It is these various socio-economic changes that have provided the cultural context for the huge explosion in recorded crime that has occurred during the past 40 years. It will be informative to consider that phenomenon more closely.

Four closely interconnected explanations – but some more contested than others – can be proposed to explain this huge increase in crime. A relatively uncontested explanation observes the huge increase in opportunity provided by the growth of the consumer soci-ety. It is instructive in this context that 94% of all notifiable offences recorded by the police are against property[89] and ownership of consumer durables is widespread.[90] A fur-ther relatively uncontested explanation points to the 'breakdown in informal social con-trols' that has occurred in society. Norman Dennis in his various accounts draws attention to the decline in the traditional nuclear family and the rise of the single-parent family.[91] Certainly, it is a disturbing reality that many children – predominantly from the workless classes – now grow up without experiencing positive male role models. Others have ar-gued that detached from their traditional role of the 'breadwinner', many young men have little to offer women and their children long-term, other than the violence and sexual abuse that often characterised traditional working-class life.[92] Consequently, they have become excluded from the informal social controls of employment, dependents and re-spectable peer group pressure that have traditionally diverted young people from criminal behaviour.[93] For some, this ever-increasing group of excluded young men are an 'underclass' and their criminal and general antisocial behaviour terrorises the neighbour-hoods in which they live.[94]

A further closely interconnected but less widely voiced explanation observes the disinte-gration of the traditional collective working-class culture and the triumph of competitive-ness and entrepreneurialism.[95] The 'go for it' philosophy of the enterprise culture has penetrated the whole social structure, from the board rooms of big business, to the dealing rooms of international finance capital, to politicians demanding cash to ask questions in the House of Commons, to higher education institutions selling courses for profit, to long-term benefit claimants having a 'nice little earner on the side', to youths carrying out robberies on the street or committing burglaries. Everyone is an entrepreneur now. The boundaries between many legitimate and illegitimate business activities are increasingly blurred.[96] Morality is indeed ambiguous.

The writings of Emile Durkheim suggest that he would have been critical of the 'unbridled egoism' that has underpinned the lives and transactions of people during the past 20 years. He would have considered the very idea that a stable society could be built on the basis of a series of private exchanges between individuals – the argument of the freemarketeers and utilitarians who enjoyed a renaissance during that period – plainly absurd. Quite the contrary. For Durkheim the need for efficient regulation and state intervention is greater at times of rapid social change – like that experienced in the UK during the 1980s and 1990s – because new forms of control have not evolved sufficiently to replace the older, and now less appropriate, means of maintaining solidarity. In such a period, society is in a state of normlessness which Durkheim described as 'anomie'.[97]

For Durkheim, anomie is characterised by a breakdown in norms and common understandings within a society. Without external controls, a human being has unlimited needs. Society has to regulate these needs by indicating suitable rewards. Problematically, during a period of economic upheaval, society cannot exert controls on the aspirations of people. During a depression, people are forced to lower their sights, a situation which some will find intolerable. When there is a sudden improvement in economic conditions, social equilibrium also breaks down. There is no limit on aspirations:

> Individual demands and appetites become unregulated and 'egoism' prevails, ultimately even developing its own individualistic normative structure, at a variance to that previously held by wider society.[98]

This observation leads us to our final closely interconnected but again less widely voiced explanation of the huge explosion in crime that has occurred during the past 40 years. The mass working-class culture of modernity was based on the similarity of existence described earlier in this essay. The increasingly organic consumer society has brought spending power, opportunities, and with it new and diverse groups with subjective and varied interests which have often set them against the traditions of their parent communities. Young people, of course, have been in the vanguard of this change.

The development of a group identity through an association with others who share a particular taste in music and clothes has been an important part of the transition to adulthood for many young people since the beginnings of the consumer society. The structural changes that have occurred in society during the past 20 years have, however, encouraged greater reliance on such associations into adulthood.[99] Where the opportunity for identity development through work and family has become more difficult to attain, then group identity associated with wider subcultural groups may become all the more important.

Early studies in the USA[100] and the UK[101] had considered youth subculture-linked deviance to be a working-class issue associated with economic deprivation or status deprivation. More recent studies suggest that such experiences are now widespread and are no longer confined to the working classes.[102] Significantly, these groups contain many generally law-abiding, articulate, educated citizens who *occasionally* engage in deviant and illegal activity. For example, the smoking of cannabis is widespread among middle-class professionals[103] and recent research has suggested that 87% of ravers take Ecstasy regularly.[104] Recreational drug use is now apparently the norm for many young people. Where the older generation used to get drunk at the pub on a Friday or Saturday night, many young people apparently now consume a few Es instead.[105]

In summary, it has been argued in this section that it is extremely unlikely that crime can be reduced by using the police service as a blunt instrument with which to restore the unobtainable moral certainties of modern society. Frankly, we should not be surprised that crime has exploded during the past 40 years. During that period the UK has become substantially more prosperous than at any time in its history while at the same time that wealth has not been equally shared. Significantly, the qualitative experience of poverty and unemployment today is substantially different than in the past.

These socio-economic changes have provided the cultural context for the huge explosion in recorded crime. First, the consumer society has provided a greatly increased opportunity for economic crime. Second, there has been a breakdown in the old informal social controls that served to socialise the young into the traditional, respectable – if somewhat flawed – working-class culture. Third, the rise of entrepreneurialism has permeated the whole social structure with a parallel increase in egoism and anomie. Fourth, young people – not only from the traditional working class – have responded to these changes by involvement in subcultural groupings where casual, but not necessarily regular, deviant behaviour such as recreational drug use is often the norm.

The contemporary UK is a diverse, *exciting* and, not necessarily, but sometimes, deviant postmodern society.[106] This is the fragmented and diverse, affluent but unequal, socio-cultural formation that offers a challenge for the contemporary police service. In the final section of this paper we will consider the applicability and suitability of proactive, confident, assertive policing strategies in that socio-cultural context.

Conclusions – policing and postmodern society revisited

Emile Durkheim observed that definitions of crime and deviance establish the moral boundaries of society. Deviance can, therefore, supply a springboard for progressive social change by challenging the accepted social order. We might like to reflect on the reality that contemporary societies with little crime tend to be rather sterile, repressive and uninspiring places.[107] More tolerant and socially progressive societies seem to be much more interesting and forward-looking. Such thinking, implicit but rarely articulated, allied with the rather surprisingly sustained influence of labelling theories, where it is argued

that once a person is criminalised by the criminal justice process they will
motivation to continue on a criminal career,[108] has certainly encourag
interventionist trend in responding to much 'minor' criminal behaviour, in
vandalism and incivilities on the streets.

Without doubt – as we identified above – there has been a rather convenient convergence
between this liberal/libertarian criminal justice discourse and the economic interests of a
police management with limited resources. The unintended consequences of this unspo-
ken and unofficial *de facto* non-interventionist policing policy have seen the parameters
of 'acceptable' deviance shifted beyond a point acceptable to large numbers of the public.
Thus, zero tolerance-style policing strategies that have sought to reclaim the streets for
'the decent citizen' have coincided neatly with a very widespread public enthusiasm to
push back the boundaries of public deviancy. Hence, the first proposition presented at the
outset of this essay which states that there is a general consumer demand in society for a
highly visible police presence on the streets. Significantly, this demand exists among all
ethnic and interest groups.

On the other hand, strategies to help restore the moral contours of modernity – a proud,
homogeneous, inward-looking, working-class mechanical solidarity and culture – are
likely to be widely met with contempt, derision and even social unrest in many parts of
society. Consequently, the second proposition observes that the nature of the police presence on the streets and any subsequent intervention needs to be sensitive to the requirements of local people in order to achieve legitimacy within that community.

The police service can only be successful if its activities are legitimate in the eyes of the
communities it seeks to serve. Failure to achieve this endorsement will be expressed in
two closely linked and highly damaging forms of dissent. First, there will be an escalation
in widespread public disorder. It will of course be recognised that disorder comes in
different forms and that these can be placed at different points on a continuum of seriousness. There are the full-blown riots that have occurred both in the inner cities, on the
outer-estates[109] and at public rallies and protests against unpopular political policies.[110] At
the other end of the continuum there is the smaller scale disorder that occurs on a regular
basis on a Friday and Saturday night throughout the country in towns and cities – big and
small – as the pubs and clubs empty their clientele onto the street.[111]

The second form of dissent will involve a tacit withdrawal of help and assistance to the
police service. The process described in this essay where black people choose loyalty to
their ethnic group against helping to target criminal and anti-social elements in their
communities will be more widely generalised. Indeed, this is probably already the case in
diverse communities throughout society. Certainly, many people who have attended professional football matches as spectators during the past 20 years will have witnessed
examples of unprofessional behaviour on the part of members of the police service. These
events leave lasting memories.

There are obviously serious implications for the contemporary police service and these
have been noted both by policing academics and serving police officers. Indeed, many of

the observations contained in this paper are familiar to serving police officers of all ranks, albeit sometimes articulated in less academic language. This recognition has led increasingly to strategies of withdrawal and tolerance that have been dressed up and articulated by a contemporary public relations-obsessed police service as being consumer-friendly and liberal. In the meantime, the number of recorded criminal offences – and an even greater number declared to crime surveys – increases ever upwards, except for the occasional statistical blip, while the police detection rate plummets ever downwards.[112] It appears that the contemporary police service is markedly unsuccessful at both preventing crime and catching criminals while no longer providing the general policing presence on the streets that the great majority of the public want.[113]

It is the central contention of this paper that there is a widespread demand for a proactive, confident, assertive, police service that is highly visible on the streets. We may live in a diverse and fragmented society – with diverse interests and diverse points of view – but there is a widespread demand for a positive response to the crime problem. At least two positive lessons can be learned from the recent experience of New York City. First, coalitions of support can be gained from diverse communities for positive initiatives to tackle crime. Second, those initiatives are likely to be successful if they are perceived as being 'fair'. Policing strategies that target people purely because they are black, for example, will fail to gain the support of the wider community and alienate large sections of a group of people who want and demand fair and honest policing. Hence, the third proposition presented at the outset of this essay which proposes that widely legitimated policing strategies can be assertive as long as they are perceived as 'fair'.

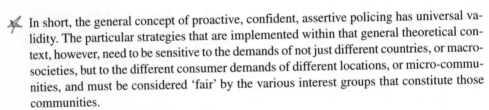

In short, the general concept of proactive, confident, assertive policing has universal validity. The particular strategies that are implemented within that general theoretical context, however, need to be sensitive to the demands of not just different countries, or macro-societies, but to the different consumer demands of different locations, or micro-communities, and must be considered 'fair' by the various interest groups that constitute those communities.

Notes

1   It should be noted that at no time am I referring to the particular policing situation in Northern Ireland.

2   The term soundbite means a short snappy phrase which is picked up on and used by the media.

3   Wilson, J.Q. and Kelling, G.L. (1982) Broken Windows. *Atlantic Monthly*, March, 1982, pp 29-38. George Kelling has distanced himself from the notion of zero tolerance because, as he rightly observes, it fails to acknowledge the 'highly discretionary nature of good policing'. Quoted in Howe, S. (1997) Kelling's Law. *Policing Today*, December, p 17.

4   See Bratton, W.J. (1997) Crime is Down in New York City: Blame the Police. In Dennis, N. (ed.) *Zero Tolerance: Policing a Free Society*. London: Institute for Economic Affairs.

5   See Dennis, N. and Mallon, R. (1997) Confident Policing in Hartlepool. In Dennis (ed.), op cit.

6   Official crime statistics are of course problematic and there are a number of reasons why these cannot be considered an accurate representation of the true level of crime in a society. For an introduction to this notion, see Maguire, M. (1997) Crime Statistics, Patterns, and Trends: Changing Perceptions and their Implications. In Maguire, M., Morgan, R. and Reiner R. (eds) *The Oxford Handbook of Criminology*. Oxford: Clarendon Press.

7   Bratton, op cit, p 29.

8   Dennis and Mallon, op cit, p 62.

9   Lea, J. and Young, J. (1984) *What is to be Done about Law and Order?* Harmondsworth: Penguin, p 177.

10 Scarman, Lord, (1981) *The Brixton Disorders 10 - 12 April 1981: Report of an Inquiry by the Rt Hon. the Lord Scarman, OBE*. London: HMSO.

11 Wilson and Kelling, op cit. President Ronald Reagan appointed Professor Wilson as his special adviser on crime.

12 Wilson, J.Q. (1975) *Thinking About Crime*. New York: Basic Books.

13 Lea and Young, op cit.

14 Scarman, op cit, p 14.

15 Ibid.

16 For an excellent overview of the arguments for comprehensive community partnership against crime, see Pease, K. (1997) Crime Prevention. In Maguire et al (eds), op cit.

17 McLaughlin, E. (1996) Police, Policing and Policework. In McLaughlin, E. and Muncie, J. (eds) *Controlling Crime*. London: Sage in Association with the Open University.

18 Oxford, K. (1982) Community Policing: Looking for a Definition. *Police Officer*, July.

19 Smith, D. (1987) The Police and Community. In Wilmott, P. (ed.) *Policing the Community*. London: Policy Studies Institute.

20 Ibid.

21 Ibid.

22 Morgan, R. (1997) Swept Along by Zero Option. *The Guardian,* 22 January. See also Crowther, C. (1998) 'Policing The Excluded Society' in this volume.

23 See, for example, Morgan, R. and Newburn, T. (1997) *The Future of Policing*. Oxford: Clarendon Press.

24 See ibid.

25 Ibid.

26 See Bayley, D. (1994) *Police for the Future*. New York: Oxford University Press.

27 See Bratton, op cit; Dennis and Mallon, op cit.

28 In the UK in particular, there had been a whole series of localised initiatives. For example 'Operation Bumblebee' introduced by the Metropolitan Police to target burglars operating in London.

29 Friedmann, R.R. (1992) *Community Policing: Comparative Perspectives and Prospects*. London: Harvester Wheatsheaf.

30 Ibid, p 26.

31 NYPD squad cars carried advertisements in their back windows at the time offering rewards of $10,000 for information leading to the arrest of people who had shot police officers.

32 See Bratton, op cit, p 34.

33 NY1, a 24-hour television news station serving New York City.

34 Youths who extort money from stationary car drivers by 'washing' their car windows. See Kelling, G.L. and Coles, C.M. (1996) *Fixing Broken Windows: Restoring Order and Reducing Crime in Our Communities*. New York: The Free Press.

35 Bratton, op cit.

36 Mayor Giuliani was, at that time, embroiled in a plan to slash NYC's education budget and was involved in an extensive ongoing battle with Schools Chancellor, Ramon Cortez. Cortez later resigned and Giuliani's budget proposals were adopted by the City Council.

37 Bratton, op cit.

38 Nelken, D. (ed.) (1994) *The Futures of Criminology*, London: Sage; Morrison, W. (1995) *Theoretical Criminology: From Modernity to Post Modernism*. London: Cavendish.

39 For an excellent account, see Harvey, D. (1989) *The Condition of Postmodernity: An Enquiry into the Origins of Cultural Change*. Oxford: Basil Blackwell.

40 See Althusser, L. (1969) *For Marx*. London: Allen Lane. Giddens, A. (1989) *Sociology*, Oxford: Polity Press, provides an introduction to these comprehensive debates.

41 See, for example, Bunyan, T. (1976) *The Political Police in Britain*. London: Quartet; Cohen, P. (1979) *Policing the Working Class City*. In Fine, B. Kinsey, R. Lea, J. Picciotto, S. and Young, J. (eds) *Capitalism and the Rule of Law*. London: Hutchinson; Scraton, P. (1985) *The State of the Police*. London: Pluto; Storch, R. (1975) The Plague of Blue Locusts: Police Reform and Popular Resistance in Northern England 1840-1857. *International Review of Social History*. Vol. 20, No. 1, pp 61-90.

42 Lyotard, J.-F. (1984) *The Postmodern Condition: A Report on Knowledge*. Manchester: Man-

chester University Press. The idea of the postmodern involves claims that modernist features of society are under challenge. This can be seen in the realm of culture, where self-proclaimed modern thinkers and artists were challenged from the mid-1960s by anti-modernist ideas which attacked the dehumanisation of modern society (see for example, Marcuse, H. (1964) *One Dimensional Man*. Boston: Beacon). Concerns that were reflected in the field of the social sciences by the emergence of radical efforts to challenge orthodox, positivist forms of thought and reject their claims to objective scientific status (see, for example, Becker, H. (1963) *Outsiders: Studies in the Sociology of Deviance*. New York: Free Press).

43 See Harvey, op cit.

44 Giddens, A. (1994) *Beyond Left and Right*. Cambridge: Polity.

45 Bratton, op cit, p 31.

46 Pearce, D. and Harrison, J. (1997) 'Broken Windows' - NYPD Blues. *Police*, December, p 11.

47 Ibid.

48 See ibid; Kelling and Coles, op cit.

49 Quoted in Pearce and Harrison, op cit.

50 Ibid.

51 Ibid.

52 See ibid; Kelling and Coles, op cit.

53 See, for example, Morgan, op cit; Read, S. (1997) Below Zero. *Police Review*, 17 January.

54 NY1 Internet Service, 4 November 1997.

55 Ibid. Giuliani became the first Republican Mayor in 56 years to win a second term. He captured 57% of the vote, while Democrat challenger Ruth Messinger got 41%. In other electoral battles in the city Democrat Alan Hevesi won re-election as City Comptroller over his Republican challenger by a margin of over 50%. In the race to replace Ruth Messinger as Manhattan Borough President, Democrat C. Virginia Fields beat Republican Abe Hirschfeld by almost 50 points.

56 Read, op cit.

57 See Lea and Young, op cit; Matthews, R. and Young, J. (eds) (1986) *Confronting Crime*. London: Sage; Matthews, R. and Young, J. (eds) (1992) *Issues in Realist Criminology*. London: Sage; Young, J. (1994) Incessant Chatter: Recent Paradigms in Criminology. In Maguire et al (eds), op cit.

58 See, for example, Norris, C., Fielding, N., Kemp, C. and Fielding, J. (1992) Black and Blue: An Analysis of the Influence of Race on Being Stopped by the Police. *British Journal of Sociology*. Vol. 43, No. 2, pp 207-24; Bucke, T. (1995) *Policing and the Public: Findings from the 1994 British Crime Survey*. Home Office Research and Statistics Department, Research Findings No. 28. London: Home Office.

59 Scarman, op cit.

60 According to the Fiscal Policy Institute, New York has the most extreme income distribution in the United States between the upper and lower classes. Families at the top fifth of the income spectrum earned more than $132,000 dollars, while families at the bottom fifth earned less than $7,000 dollars. The middle fifth earned about $39,000. Source: NY1 Internet Service, 18th December, 1997.

61 The numbers of homicides in New York City for the years 1994, 1995 and 1996 were as follows:

1994	1995	1996
1,582	1,182	983

62 See Miller, J., cited in Chaudhary, V. and Walker, M. (1996) The Petty Crime War. *The Guardian,* 21 November.

63 It is an interesting fact that Harlem, a predominantly black area of New York City, has more churches than any other area in the God-fearing USA.

64 Sherman, L.W. (1983) After the Riots: Police and Minorities in the United States, 1970-80. In Glazer, N. and Young, K. (eds) *Ethnic Pluralism and Public Policy*. London: Heinemann.

65 Rodney King, a black man who was severely beaten by a group of white police officers in the course of arresting him in Los Angeles in 1991. Clear evidence of that beating was provided by amateur video tape played at the first trial of the four police officers in 1992, but in spite of this an all-white jury acquitted them. Smith, D.J. (1997) Ethnic Origins, Crime and Criminal Justice. In Maguire et al, op cit.

66 Bratton, op cit.

67 A number of police officers had gone to a policing convention in Washington DC, had got drunk and trashed their hotel. Another group had gone to a resort in New Jersey while off-duty and had become involved in a bar-room brawl. Commissioner Bratton had summarily dismissed all those involved.

68 Carlin, J. (1997) New York's Finest Accused of Brutality. *The Independent,* 18 August, p 10.

69 Professor Norman Dennis is - at the time of writing - Guest Fellow at the Department of Religious Studies at the University of Newcastle-upon-Tyne. Superintendent Ray Mallon is currently head of crime control at Middlesbrough, Cleveland and is credited with introducing a variant of zero tolerance-style policing, the 'Here and Now', to Cleveland Constabulary.

70 Dennis, N. and Mallon, R. (1997) Crime and Culture in Hartlepool. In Dennis, N. (ed.), op cit.

71 Ibid. See also Dennis, N. and Erdos, G. (1992) *Families Without Fatherhood*. London: Institute of Economic Affairs.

72 Leonard, M. (1997) *Britain: Renewing Our Identity*. London: Demos.

73 One of the finest examples of the genre was written by Dennis, N., with Henriques, F. and Slaughter, C. (1956) *Coal is Our Life*, London: Eyre & Spottiswoode.

74 Any good introductory sociology textbook contains this information. It is not necessary to promote any one over another here.

75 Durkheim, E. (1964, originally 1893) *The Division of Labour in Society*. New York and London: Free Press/Macmillan.

76 Pearson, G. (1983) *Hooligan: A History of Respectable Fears*. London: Macmillan; Pearson, G. (1994) Youth Crime. In Maguire et al (eds), op cit.

77 Ibid, p 1165.

78 Pearson (1983), op cit.

79 Anyone doubting that this is the case should consult the Boulting Brothers' excellent film version of Graham Greene's *Brighton Rock* for a study in the extremely limited aspirations of 1940s 'gangsters' in the UK. Geoffrey Pearson provides us with the example of press reports of soccer-related violence during the 1890s that could easily have described events at a match during the 1970s. See Pearson (1983), op cit. Perhaps there will always be a strong correlation between the consumption of strong alcohol, poor refereeing and attempted attacks on the latter. The organised and structured soccer-related violence conducted by a small minority of highly geographically and often internationally mobile 'football hooligans' is a very contemporary and qualitatively different matter. See Burke, R. and Sunley, R. (1996) *'Hanging Out' in the 1990s: Young People and the Postmodern Condition*. Occasional Paper 11, COP Series. Leicester: Scarman Centre for the Study of Public Order, University of Leicester; Burke, R. and Sunley R. (1998, forthcoming) Youth Subcultures in Contemporary Britain. In Hazelhurst, K. (ed.) *Gangs and Youth Subcultures: International Exploration*. Justice and Reform, Vol. 4. New Jersey: Transaction Press.

80 An important exception is Japan. See Braithwaite, J. (1989) *Crime, Shame and Reintegration*, Cambridge: Cambridge University Press for an interesting discusssion of why this is the case.

81 There have of course been reductions in the number of recorded crimes in recent years. These have been extremely small decreases in the context of the previous huge rises and the official crime figures remain far greater than was the case in 1955. The various British Crime Surveys suggest that the incidence of crime is far higher than recorded in the official figures. Mayhew, P. and Hough, M. (1989) The British Crime Survey: Origins and Impact. In Maguire, M. and Pointing, J. (eds) *Victims of Crime: A New Deal?* Milton Keynes: Open University Press; Mayhew, P., Elliott, D. and Dowds, L. (1989) *The British Crime Survey*. Home Office Research Study 111. London: HMSO.

82 Durkheim, op cit.

83 Northcott, J. (1991) *Britain in 2010*. London: Policy Studies Institute.

84 'McJobs': 'A low-pay, low-prestige, low-dignity, low-benefit, no-future job in the service sector. Frequently considered a satisfying career choice by people who have never held one'. Coupland, D. (1992) *Generation X: Tales for an Accelerated Culture*. London: Abacus, p 6.

85   Morgan and Newburn, op cit, p 13.

86   Joseph Rowntree Foundation (1995) *Income and Wealth: Report of the JRF Inquiry Group, Summary.* York: Joseph Rowntree. Cited in Morgan and Newburn, op cit, p 13.

87   My memory tells me that some years ago Central TV were the first UK television company to introduce 24-hour viewing on the grounds that the unemployed had no reason to go to bed early. For what other reason would the company regularly broadcast a programme entitled 'Central Job Finder' at 4.30 am?

88   Dennis and Erdos, op cit; Dennis, N. and Mallon, R. (1997) Confident Policing in Hartlepool. In Dennis (ed.), op cit; Dennis, N. and Mallon, R. (1997) Crime and Culture in Hartlepool. In Dennis (ed.), op cit.

89   Barclay, G.C. (1995) *The Criminal Justice System in England and Wales 1995.* London: Home Office, Research and Statistics Department. Morgan and Newburn, op cit, p 33 note that whereas motor vehicles were in very short supply 40 years ago they now account for upwards of one quarter of all recorded crime.

90   In the contemporary UK telephones and televisions are considered necessities and all but the very poorest own a video recorder.

91   Dennis and Erdos, op cit; Dennis and Mallon (1997) Crime and Culture in Hartlepool. In Dennis (ed.), op cit.

92   Campbell, B. (1993) *Goliath: Britain's Dangerous Places.* London: Methuen. This paper has chosen to emphasise economically motivated crime. It is important, however, that we acknowledge the influence of feminism - in particular - in the redefining of previously, often secret, but relatively unproblematic practices, such as domestic violence and child abuse, as criminal offences.

93   The peak age for offending was 17-19 years for males and 15 years for females in 1993. This is based upon the number of offenders either convicted by the courts or cautioned by the police for indictable offences. Barclay, op cit.

94   Ibid.

95   This is a process usually associated with the various Conservative governments led by Margaret Thatcher and John Major. However, the trend has been very much in place since the 1950s. Their economic policies and legitimating philosophy merely speeded up the process.

96   See Hobbs, D. (1988) *Doing the Business: Entrepreneurship, the Working Class and Detectives in East London.* Oxford: Clarendon Press; Hobbs, D. (1994) Professional and Organised Crime in Britain. In Maguire et al (eds), op cit; Hobbs, D. (1995) *Bad Business.* Oxford: Oxford University Press.

97   Durkheim, op cit, p 228.

98   Heathcote, R. (1981) Social Disorganisation. In Fitzgerald, M., McLennan, G. and Pawson, J. (eds) *Crime and Society: Readings in History and Theory.* Milton Keynes: Open University Press/Routledge and Kegan Paul, p 347.

99   See Burke and Sunley (1996), op cit; Burke and Sunley (1998, forthcoming), op cit.

100   See, for example, Cloward, R.A. and Ohlin, L.E. (1960) *Delinquency and Opportunity: A Theory of Delinquent Gangs*. New York: Free Press; Cohen, A.K. (1955) *Delinquent Boys: The Culture of the Gang*. New York: Free Press; Miller, W.R. (1958) Lower Class Culture as a Generating Milieu of Gang Delinquency. *Journal of Social Issues*, 14, pp 5-19.

101   Downes, D. (1966) *The Delinquent Solution*. London: Routledge and Kegan Paul; Parker, H. (1974) *View From the Boys*. Newton Abbot: David and Charles; Pryce, K. (1979) *Endless Pressure: A Study of West Indian Life-Styles in Bristol*. Harmondsworth: Penguin.

102   For example, 'lager-louts', 'townies', new-style football 'crews' (old-style football hooligans), 'crusties', 'ganstas' and 'ravers' - see Burke and Sunley (1996), op cit; Burke and Sunley (1998 forthcoming), op cit.

103   *The Independent on Sunday* is currently conducting an extremely high-profile campaign to legalise cannabis. This appears to be a campaign predominantly promoted and supported by the professional middle class.

104   Mike Goodman, the director of Release, quoted by Bennetto, J. (1997) Sex, Drugs and Club Life Send Britain's Youth Raving for More, *The Independent*, 6 August.

105   Ibid.

106   A recent study conducted by the think-tank Demos and funded by the Design Council implored the 'new-style' UK government led by Tony Blair to challenge the negative outdated image of the country that exists in parts of the world: an image of unfriendly and arrogant people, sloppy and inedible food, poverty, draughty houses and ubiquitous rituals. We should take note that the postmodern consumer society has produced a number of Nobel prizes for science second only to the United States and one-fifth of all post-war inventions in the world. British design, fashion and music are its strongest export sector with a £1.1 billion turnover in 1996 and are global pacesetters. The crime rate may have exploded during the past 40 years, but it is also a society which thrives on diversity and uses it constantly to renew and re-energise itself. Britain has over 3 million people who describe themselves as non-white and houses most of the world's religions. Leonard, op cit.

107   Some have identified societies with low crime rates - such as Japan and the 'tiger economies' of the Pacific rim - to be 'strong on perspiration but short on inspiration'. *The Independent on Sunday,* 17 August, 1997, p 24.

108   See, for example, Becker, op cit; Lemert, E. (1967) *Human Deviance, Social Problems and Social Control*. Englewood Cliffs, NJ: Prentice Hall; Schur, E. (1971) *Labelling Deviant Behaviour: Its Sociological Implications*. New York: Harper and Row. Rock, P. (1973) *Deviant Behaviour*. London: Hutchinson.

109   Those large housing estates located on the perimeters of all large towns and cities built to house the workforce of modernity but which now function as dumping grounds and open prisons for the excluded of contemporary society.

110   For example, the 'poll tax' riots that occurred in the late 1980s against the unpopular community charge local government tax introduced by the Conservative government led by Margaret Thatcher.

111   In reality, this is in many ways a more serious manifestation of disorder than a full-blown riot because such events have become so common and are readily accepted by many (particularly young) people as a 'normal' part of life.

112   In 1993, the police recorded 5.5. million notifiable offences, of which 94% were against property, 5% were violent and the remaining 1% were other types of crime. The total number of crimes recorded in 1993 was 1% lower than in 1992. This was the first fall in the annual figures since 1988 and compares with a 5.5% annual average increase over the last ten years.

From *The 1994 British Crime Survey* based upon interviews with households, estimates suggest that the increases in actual crime have been lower than recorded by the police, with only one quarter of all crime recorded by the police.

In 1993, 25% of all offences were cleared up by the police, compared with 26% in 1992 and 32% in 1986. For offences cleared up in 1993, 46% resulted in an offender being charged or summoned for an offence, 15% in a caution, 14% were offences taken into consideration, 17% followed interviews with convicted prisoners and in 9% of cases no further action was taken.

Source: Barclay, op cit.

113   See Morgan and Newburn, op cit.

Chapter 3

A Question of Confidence: Zero Tolera and Problem-Oriented Policing

Terry Romeanes[1]

Introduction

Cleveland Constabulary is one of the few police forces in the UK to have explicitly used 'zero tolerance'-style policing strategies[2] and it has subsequently received a considerable amount of publicity. Since this style of policing was first introduced in the Police District of Hartlepool during 1994 the number of recorded offences in that town has been halved. In the District of Middlesbrough reported crime was reduced by one–fifth within six weeks of its introduction in 1996. Before Christmas of that year an average of 75 crimes (20 of these were burglaries) were committed each day; by February 1997 the comparable figures were 60 and 12 respectively.[3] Zero tolerance-style strategies are, however, only part of the policing approach in Cleveland.

It is the purpose of this paper to outline and discuss recent policing policies introduced by the Cleveland Constabulary and to dispel much of the recent hype and many of the myths that have developed which tend to lead many to reach the conclusion that 'zero tolerance' and 'problem-oriented policing' are incompatible philosophies.[4] For us, they are not only compatible but part of a community-based policing tradition in the UK from which we have become diverted during the past 30 years.

In Cleveland, 'zero tolerance' policing as we understand it has allowed officers to take back the streets. When you get them back the question becomes one of what you are going to do with them. In Cleveland the answer lies in the longer-term strategies of problem-oriented policing, crime prevention and community safety. It is the implementation of these strategies that maintains the confidence of the public in their organisation.

The Cleveland Constabulary is a modern, forward-thinking organisation which has achieved a deserved reputation for its information technology systems and its devolved resource management philosophy. Furthermore, it provides an excellent example of 'bottom-up' policing achieved through the introduction of a system of user, service and policy groups which determine the three main strategies that drive the ce. These are:

- the crime strategy;
- the operations strategy;
- the development strategy.

These contain subsidiary strategies created to interlock in a flexible manner to meet the varied policing demands of the area. It is within the operations strategy that the zero tolerance and problem-oriented policing strategies are located. These merit consideration – first, zero tolerance.

Zero tolerance

In 1992 I took command of Hartlepool Police District. It was clear at the time that the main concern of the public was the 'fear of crime': not crime itself, but the fear of it. This was a perception – as opposed to reality – nurtured by a hostile local press and the lack of a visible presence of uniformed police officers on the streets.

My primary concern was to get the policing structure right and move from a purely, and largely ineffectual, responsive system based on a central police station to a locally-based system of highly visible community policing teams. This was achieved through a partnership with the local authority, Hartlepool Borough Council, who provided offices, free of any cost to the force, to house the community policing teams designated to work in the four most problematic areas of the Borough. Detective officers returning to uniform on tenure were drafted into each of the teams to provide investigatory expertise. A management team was put together that shared my policing philosophy and this included the appointment of a new crime manager, a young Detective Chief Inspector, Ray Mallon, whom I had worked with previously on the Regional Crime Squad, and Chief Inspector Geoff Lee, an experienced uniformed officer. We discussed how we might reduce crime, and more importantly the fear of crime, and the outcome was a policy of targeting burglars through their involvement in minor offences. It was this strategy that came to be labelled by the media 'zero tolerance'.

A central and widely acknowledged role for the police is the detection of crimes and apprehension of suspects, but there are two other roles at least as important that had somehow lost their prominence – reducing the number of crimes committed and recovering control of the streets on behalf of the law-abiding population. We decided to tackle these issues in Hartlepool by simply paying attention to, not ignoring, antisocial behaviour and 'nuisance crime'. This 'zero tolerance' strategy would involve the police regaining control of the streets by controlling minor situations. A central intention was to regain public confidence in its police service – it would be 'confident policing'.

Central to this strategy was the removal of anonymity from delinquents. One of the sources of frustration among local people was that victims often knew who the perpetrators of crimes against them were and 'the authorities' seemed incapable of doing anything about it. Police officers were to tackle this anonymity by getting to know criminals and making it clear that they knew them. In short, the confident policing of low-order offences involves letting the youth know that if he or she goes too far the chances are that someone will identify them as the offender. This was one focus of the new crime strategy.

The other focus was on house burglary, which evidence has shown to be the offence that the public fear the most.[5] Most burglars are always on the lookout for the opportunity to commit an offence. Consequently, if the police can restrain the house burglar, all the other offences he or she would normally have committed if they had been at liberty are reduced as well.[6] Furthermore, by the 1990s the only volume-crime offender normally sent to prison was the convicted burglar. Consequently, if they are caught and convicted they are put completely out of circulation. In short, by concentrating on the burglar there would be a considerable reduction in all criminal activity in the town.

The crime strategy included the cultivation of informants, and generally encouraging information-based action.[7] With rising confidence in the police, the public became more forthcoming and constables themselves fed back their own direct knowledge from their patrols. Central to the strategy was the implementation of these tactics in a highly professional manner within the law and the traditional customs and experiences of British policing. The style of management was that of 'winning without cheating, winning within the rules'. Teamwork depended on specialisation on the one hand, and shared knowledge and co-ordination on the other. Team motivation and sharing knowledge were fostered during regular meetings. The intelligence branch was put at the centre of operations – around this centre were the crime desk, receiving information and passing it to the intelligence branch for dissemination throughout the system, the uniform branch, the local beat officers, CID, and the specialised field officers. Success depended upon both uniform and CID officers sharing the same goals.

Zero tolerance or 'confident policing' can be summarised as: the 'what' (the strategy to be used); the 'how' (the tactics to be used); and the 'who' (the four sets of people whose co-operation is needed to secure the strategy and the tactics: the workforce, the management, the media and the public). Zero tolerance is the 'here and now' strategy, the short-term strategy of the Cleveland Constabulary. The long-term strategy is 'problem-oriented policing'. Critics argue that the two are incompatible:

> the former implies emphasis on strong law enforcement and the use of the formal criminal justice system; the latter sees the police using a much wider variety of tactics to achieve their objectives, working closely in harmony with the local community and agencies, seeking the underlying causes of problems and trying to solve them for the longer term, rather than merely dealing superficially with the symptoms.[8]

In fact, the two strategies are entirely compatible: zero tolerance provides the preconditions for problem-oriented policing. In the words of Ray Mallon, 'We need to clear the alligators out of the pond before we can go swimming'.

Problem-oriented policing

Background

The Teesside area has, like many others areas of the UK, been the subject of the Thatcherite Revolution. It has, in the past 30 years, lost most of its traditional heavy industries of iron, steel and shipbuilding. Even the industrial base of petrochemicals, once dominated by ICI, has been the subject of considerable restructuring. The Table below shows that un-employment and other indices of social change have placed ever-increasing demands upon the police.

Table: Indices of social change in Cleveland 1975 – 1995

Indices of social change		%
Unemployment	+	119.7
Single-parent families	+	129.0
Crime	+	176.0
Calls to the police	+	254.0

During that time the population has remained relatively constant at around 550,000, so these figures represent real increases. During this period, police resources, in real terms, rose by only 6.5%.

These increases in consumer demand stretched resources to the limit and forced from us a response of becoming more centralised, with the parallel consequence of moving us further away from our community roots. Comments from police officers to members of the public such as 'There is nothing that I can do about it' and 'I'm sorry, it's nothing to do with the police' became commonplace. This situation was anathema to older officers but, like it or not, was now commonplace to a whole generation of officers who knew nothing else.

This increase in consumer demand was understandable in view of the increased demands on a modern police service – an increase from 24% to 94% in private access to the tel-ephone, the increasing expectations of a media-conscious public and the reduction, in real terms, of resources available to other agencies. The public still turned to the police in Cleveland as an agency of last resort but were concerned by what they perceived to be a reduced level of service and they were increasingly not prepared to accept the situation.

Through the community consultation process the public began demanding more officers located in their neighbourhoods to deal with quality of life issues on the streets, and this theme was strongly supported by the Police Authority. At the same time, strategies were introduced to deal with the large increases in crime being reported by members of the public. For example, we were one of the first police forces in the country to introduce crime management desks to filter out less serious offences and in doing so we were able to reduce our need to respond to crime by over 30%. This was well in advance of the Audit Commission's publication, *Helping with Enquiries: Tackling Crime Effectively*.[9]

To address the quality of life issues, in March 1996 the Cleveland Constabulary Policy Group held a special meeting to discuss the possibility of introducing 'problem-oriented' policing throughout the force. It was decided that such a strategy would need to be community-based if it were to succeed and there were four essential prerequisites to ensure that success: (i) a locally-based policing structure; (ii) devolved resource management; (iii) responsive information technology; and (iv) executive and management commitment. Each of these merits consideration since they are at the very heart of problem-oriented policing.

Locally-based policing structure

Cleveland has four police districts which are coterminous with the four local authority districts. The Chief Superintendent, supported by a uniform Superintendent, a Detective Superintendent and a Divisional Administration Officer, works extremely closely with the local authority Chief Executive. Each has a police officer working in the Chief Executive's Office as a conduit to expedite issues of mutual interest. Each Police District is divided into Community Policing Teams which cover the whole of the area. These teams are, wherever possible, aligned to Local Authority Community Councils and natural communities. Each of the Community Policing Teams is encouraged to develop strong local links at grass-roots level, sitting alongside other agencies at local community forums. Some of the teams are based in the premises of other agencies, while some have local authority employees working within their offices.

We were fortunate that the removal of Cleveland County Council in April 1996 and its replacement with four unitary authorities concentrated the main agencies under one chief executive. Furthermore, their fresh approach towards partnership with the police made them amenable to a close working relationship. What Cleveland Constabulary did was to take the need for a 'partnership' approach beyond the rhetoric of consultation and lay the foundation for joint strategy and informed decision-making.

Devolved resource management

Devolved resource management from the centre to the district level was essential to the success of the decentralisation strategy and was completed in 1994. Service Unit Managers and District Commanders in particular, as the main budget holders of the force, were now provided with complete financial freedom, within the constraints of the force strategies, to determine the policing of their area of responsibility.

Incrementally each year since 1994 the Chief Constable, Mr Barry Shaw, has apportioned a greater share of the budget to the operational arm of policing at the expense of the bureaucratic management centre. As a consequence, Cleveland Constabulary now has more police constables than at any time in its history. It is also more able to respond to change more effectively than ever before.

Responsive information technology

The highly influential US academic Herman Goldstein in his book *Problem Oriented Policing* had argued that:

> Conveying sound, accurate information is currently one of the least used but potentially most effective means the police have for responding to a wide range of problems.[10]

In short, any police service embarking on a problem-oriented policing strategy must have an information technology structure with systems that can rapidly and accurately provide data to be analysed by personnel specially trained in that area. It was decided that we would aim for two complementary but separate information technology systems to deliver problem-oriented policing. This was our Crime and Incident Pattern Analysis System (CIPAS) and Problem-Oriented Policing (POP) Administration System.

CIPAS is fully up and running across Cleveland Constabulary and is driven by our district analysts, who are all psychologists. The system shows incident, crime, stop-check patterns and information linked either on an analysis chart or displayed on a mapped background. The POP Administration System allows us to track our POP problems and produce management reports/graphs. One of the important functions of the system is to allow the creation of a best practice database, and this will grow over time.

Management commitment

At the Force Policy Group Meeting of March 1996 an unprecedented unanimous agreement was reached to introduce a problem-oriented policing strategy, and I was given the task of overseeing its introduction. From the outset it was decided that every member of the force would attend a workshop at which the philosophy of the policy would be discussed and inculcated into the thinking of everyone – uniform branch and CID, police and civilian support staff.

In all, 214 workshops have been held and 84% have been introduced by the Chief Constable, or an officer of ACPO (Association of Chief Police Officers) rank. Each Executive Officer team in each of the four District Councils has had a presentation, as have each of the Community Consultative Groups. The Chief Constable sat alongside the Chairman of the Police Authority and the Chief Executive of Stockton Borough Council at a regional press launch. There is total commitment for community-based problem-oriented policing within the executive and senior management of Cleveland Constabulary. We were now ready for the introduction of the strategy into the force area.

The introduction of problem-oriented policing

The process of introducing problem-oriented policing in the Cleveland Constabulary commenced in April 1996 under the Successful Project Management System (SPM).[11] A Community Policing Team under the command of an Inspector was chosen in Billingham, a part of Stockton District, to pilot the strategy. Billingham was chosen as it was considered to have a socio-economic profile typical of Cleveland as a whole. The project commenced on 1st October 1996 and was continuously assessed until 1st April 1997 when the strategy was launched force-wide using 25 Community Policing Teams. If this larger experiment proves to be successful then it is proposed to extend the strategy throughout the force during 1998 and in 1999. In the meanwhile let us examine some examples of the achievements of problem-oriented policing in Cleveland to date.

Achievements to date

The first example involves a case where the police were being repeatedly called by residents and visitors complaining of people cycling across the pedestrianised town centre. The local council were approached and the number of complaints and wasted police resources were brought to their attention. They subsequently spent £1,300 on new measures to prevent access to cyclists, and erected new signs reminding them that they were banned under a bye-law. Police officers reinforced the message by stopping anyone riding a bike in the restricted area, cautioning him or her formally on the first occasion and prosecuting them on the second occasion (this was rarely required). These actions virtually eliminated the problem.

In another example, analysts identified that different officers had been called to the same house on 30 occasions during a three-month period by an elderly woman living alone. She was being plagued by youngsters hurling stones at her windows and smearing excrement on her walls. Extra attention was given to this case and the young people, some only 11 years of age, were traced and cautioned in front of their parents that any recurrence would result in prosecution. Again the police and the local authority worked together and the pensioner was moved to a council house nearer to her relatives where more support was available to her. A younger family was moved into the vacated property and the telephone calls ceased.

In a final example, local police officers worked with a petrol company, the Cleveland Constabulary's Architectural Liaison Officer[12] and a closed-circuit television (CCTV) engineer when analysis revealed that 48 telephone calls had been received during the course of the past 12 months from one petrol filling station. Each of these calls related to incidents where motorists had driven off without payment. On close examination it was found that the station's security system had blind spots. A few basic design changes to the forecourt and improvements to the placing of the CCTV cameras solved the problem. The Inspector in charge of the Community Policing Team stated:

> The 48 calls were four personnel days of effort which we could have well done without. By using the principles contained in problem-oriented policing, we were able to achieve a practical solution. A knock-on effect of this is that if a similar problem occurs elsewhere in the Force we have this solution recorded and we are building up a database of people who have helped us who can provide us with that knowledge again.

The list of examples is growing daily and from the 1st April 1997 problems have been registered force-wide, which provides a library source of successful strategies that can be consulted by other Community Teams facing similar problems.

What do we ultimately expect to achieve?

There are at least five basic expectations of our problem-oriented policing strategy. First, there is the anticipation that we will achieve our stated performance indicators and in particular substantially reduce the number of recorded incidents to which we have to respond, while at the same time changing the typical incident profile. Second, we aim to achieve total quality management.[13] Third, we seek a substantial increase in the status and morale of the community policing teams through a widespread recognition of the significance of their work. Fourth, we expect to achieve a far greater level of public satisfaction with the police service. Fifth, we anticipate improved multi-agency working and an end to the notion that the police can do it alone. Problem-oriented policing can clearly be seen to be part of the proactive multi-agency community partnership tradition that 'attempts to prevent crime by changing the situations in which crime occurs'.[14]

Conclusion

While problem-oriented policing is all about partnerships with other agencies and acknowledges that the police cannot do it all themselves, it would be foolish to believe that the police alone cannot, by themselves, have a considerable impact on the quality of life of the public by operating a zero tolerance approach towards crime, antisocial behaviour and quality of life offences. There are clear differences in the two strategies of zero tolerance and problem-oriented policing, but they are not incompatible. Indeed, in Cleveland we believe that they are not only complementary but that in some areas one is a necessary prerequisite for the other. The public in Cleveland have confidence in both strategies. Both are a response to community demands, so where do the intellectual difficulties lie? They lie in the fact that they are constantly being discussed in isolation by people who are unable to envisage the practical association.

Much of the difficulty lies in the preconception that the 'zero tolerance' approach in the United Kingdom must, by definition, be the same as the approaches taken in the United States and by Bill Bratton in the City of New York in particular.[15] Neither Bill Bratton nor Jack Maple, his former deputy, have ever used the expression 'zero tolerance' to describe their approach to the problems they faced when they took command of the New York Police Department.

British policing has always been community-based, but over the last 30 years we have been deflected from it. On the other hand, the United States has never really had community policing and is only now beginning to recognise the value of such an approach. In Cleveland, zero tolerance has allowed officers to take back the streets so that we can implement longer-term strategies of problem-oriented policing, crime prevention and community safety. They maintain the confidence of the public in their police force. That is not just my view, it is the overwhelming view of the officers of the Cleveland Constabulary, in whose hands the success of these strategies lie. In 1997 these strategies employed across the force contributed to a fall in crime of 18%, this was twice the national average.

Notes

1   Chief Superintendent Terry Romeanes is Force Operations Adviser to the Cleveland Constabulary.

2   Zero Tolerance: There Should be No Blind Eye to Crime. *The Times,* Leading Article, 19 November 1996.

3   Chesshyre, R. (1997) Enough is Enough. *Telegraph Magazine*, 1 March, pp 20-26.

4   See Read, S. (1997) Below Zero. *Police Review*, 17 January; Morgan, R. (1997) Swept Along by Zero Option. *The Guardian,* 22 January.

5   See Hough, M. and Mayhew, P. (1989) *Taking Account of Crime: Key Findings from the Second British Crime Survey.* London: HMSO; Mayhew, P., Maung, N. and Mirlees-Black, C. (1993) *The British Crime Survey.* London: HMSO.

6   See, for example, Bennett, T. and Wright, R. (1984) *Burglars on Burglary: Prevention and the Offender.* Aldershot: Gower; Butler, G. (1994) Commercial Burglary: What Burglars Say. In Gill, M.L. (ed.) *Crime at Work: Studies in Security and Crime Prevention.* Leicester: Perpetuity Press; Cromwell, P.F., Olson, J.N. and Avary, D. (1991) *Breaking and Entering: An Ethnographic Analysis of Burglary.* Newbury Park: Sage; Forrester, D., Chatterton, M. and Pease, K. (1988)*The Kirkholt Burglary Prevention Project, Rochdale.* CPU Paper 13. London: Home Office; Forrester, D., Frenz, S., O'Connell, M. and Pease, K. (1990) *The Kirkholt Burglary Prevention Project Phase II.* CPU paper 23. London: Home Office; Maguire, M. (1982) *Burglary in a Dwelling: the Offence, the Offender and the Victim.* Cambridge Studies in Criminology. London: Heinemann; Shover, N. (1973) The Social Organisation of Burglary. *Social Problems,* 20, pp 499-515.

7   The use of informants is a technique both invaluable and dangerous. It is recommended by Audit Commission (1993) *Helping with Enquiries: Tackling Crime Effectively,* London: Audit Commission, pp 44-6. Morgan, R. and Newburn, T. (1997) *The Future of Policing,* Oxford: Clarendon Press, pp 118-119 observe that the Audit Commission's argument is based on a somewhat naive cost-benefit analysis of the use of informants in which payments made are balanced against the number of persons arrested or the value of property recovered.

8   Pollard, C. (1997) Zero-Tolerance: Short-Term Fix, Long-Term Liability. In Dennis, N. (ed.) *Zero Tolerance: Policing a Free Society.* London: Institute for Economic Affairs, p 49.

9   Audit Commission, op cit. The approach is based on the proposition that a small proportion of offenders are prolific in their offending and that these individuals can be better targeted if crime pattern analyses and enhanced use of intelligence is brought to the centre of police operations through the establishment of a crime management desk or unit staffed by the most able officers

available. According to this model, every Basic Command Unit (BCU) should have a Field Intelligence Officer and more personnel resources should be allocated for proactive use on the basis of intelligence. See Morgan and Newburn, op cit, pp 64-65.

10 Goldstein, H. (1991) *Problem Oriented Policing*. London: McGraw Hill, p 137. For further discussion in the UK context see, for example, Burrows, J., Ekblom, P. and Heal, K. (1979) *Crime Prevention and the Police*, Home Office Research Study No. 55, London: Home Office; Clarke, R.V.G. and Hough, M. (1984) *Crime and Police Effectiveness*. London: Home Office; Johnston, V., Shapland, J. and Wiles, P. (1992) *Developing Police Crime Prevention*. CPU Paper 41. London: Home Office; Morris, P. and Heal, K. (1981) *Crime Control and the Police*. Home Office Research Study No. 67. London: Home Office.

11 The problem-oriented project (POP) took the following form: a) the decision to conduct a pilot study; b) the appointment of a project manager and team; c) liaison with the sub-district chosen for the pilot study; d) agreement with all concerned as to the time scales etc; e) design of what would count as success in order to go forward. Cleveland Constabulary believe that this methodology ensures that all concerned have the same system expectations. It also ensures that there is a separation between the project team and the staff who carry out the POP function.

12 Architectural Liaison Officers provide situational crime prevention advice on the criminogenic potential of buildings and surrounding space. For the concept of designing out crime, see, for example, Brantingham, P.J. and Brantingham, P.L. (eds) (1981) *Environmental Criminology*. Beverly Hills: Sage; Mayhew, P. (1981) Crime in Public View: Surveillance and Crime Prevention. In Brantingham and Brantingham (eds), op cit; Merry, S.E. (1981) Defensible Space Undefended. *Urban Affairs Quarterly*. 16, pp 397-422; Newman, O. (1972) *Defensible Space: Crime Prevention Through Urban Design*. New York: Macmillan; Newman, O. (1976) *Defensible Space: People and Design in the Violent City*. London: The Architectural Press; Newman, O. (1980) *Community of Interest*. New York: Anchor Press; Poyner, B. (1983) *Design Against Crime: Beyond Defensible Space*. London: Butterworths; Reiss, A.J. and Tonry, M. (eds) (1986) *Communities and Crime*. Chicago: University of Chicago Press; Webb, B. and Laycock, G. (1992) *Reducing Crime on the London Underground*. London: Home Office.

13 Total quality management is a quality control approach that emphasises organisational commitment, integration of quality improvement efforts with organisational goals, and inclusion of quality as a factor in performance appraisals. See Port, O. (1987) The Push for Quality, *Business Week*, June 8, pp 74-8. In essence, it highlights collective responsibility for the quality of products and services. It also encourages individuals in different, but related, departments to work together to improve quality. Total quality management represents a change in the way quality is perceived. Traditionally, it is has been viewed in terms of the degree of deviation from standards that is deemed allowable for products and services. In contrast, the total quality management approach is aimed at achieving zero defects, a quality mentality in which the workforce strives to a make a product or service conform exactly to desired standards. See Schroeder, R.G. (1989) *Operations Management*, 3rd edn. McGraw-Hill: New York.

14 Poyner, op cit, p 116.

15 See Bratton, W.J. (1997) Crime is Down in New York City: Blame the Police. In Dennis, N, (ed.), op cit; Hopkins Burke, R. (1998) 'A Contextualisation of Zero Tolerance Policing Strategies' and Silverman, E.B. 'Below Zero Tolerance: The New York Experience' - both in this volume.

Chapter 4

Zero Tolerance Policing: Striking the Balance, Rights and Liberties

John Wadham[1]

Introduction

'Zero tolerance' policing has different meanings, and a number of high-profile proponents of the concept – for example, William J. Bratton, the former New York Police Commissioner[2] and George Kelling, the US academic closely associated with the 'broken windows' thesis[3] – have shunned the term. On the other hand, the media and politicians have been considerably more enthusiastic about using a terminology with distinctly populist overtones; for example, the present Government stated in its General Election Manifesto:

> We will tackle the unacceptable level of anti-social behaviour and crime on our streets. Our 'zero tolerance' approach will ensure that petty criminality among young offenders is seriously addressed.[4]

Their proposed solutions are community safety orders (that will deal with 'threatening and disruptive criminal neighbours'), child protection orders (that will deal with 'young children suffering neglect by parents because they are left out on their own far too late at night') and new offences of racial harassment and increased sentences for racially-motivated offences (in order to protect ethnic minorities from intimidation). They also propose parental responsibility orders (to 'make parents face up to their responsibility for their children's misbehaviour') and reducing the number of police cautions administered (to be replaced with 'a single final warning').

It is the purpose of this paper to introduce and examine, as much as space permits, the potential civil liberties and human rights implications of 'zero tolerance' policing strategies discussed in other contributions to this volume.

Zero tolerance policing

There are at least five possible issues that are central to zero tolerance policing initiatives from a civil liberties standpoint.

- *The issue of police resources.* Given the reality of scarce resources, the introduction of zero tolerance-style strategies seems to mean that a decision must be made to allocate these resources to relatively trivial issues, since they are perceived as being much more of an everyday nuisance, rather than serious crime (for example, assaults). The essential issue is whether we wish to overburden the criminal justice system with these cases.

- *Crime on the street.* The apparent emphasis will be on street offences, to the exclusion of other kinds of crime, such as fraud or domestic violence, which are less visible.

- *The discrimination issue.* Zero tolerance policies may be discriminatory because, mostly, the poor commit street crimes. In addition, zero tolerance-style initiatives are extremely likely to lead to black young men on the street being targeted.

- *Criminalisation.* There is a considerable likelihood that zero tolerance-style initiatives will increase the numbers of people with criminal records, without any guarantee that crime levels will be reduced.

- *Accountability and democracy.* We must ask who is making these decisions and in whose interests they are being made. Essentially, we need to analyse issues of accountability and democratic control of the police service.

This paper will examine each of these issues in turn.

The issue of resources

Zero tolerance-style policing strategies have tended to be to be extremely resource-intensive. William Bratton, for example, was provided with an extra 7,000 police officers when he introduced his zero tolerance-style initiative in New York City.[5] Such staffing levels would be impossible in the UK,[6] with the consequence that resource-intensive policing of the streets in even a small well-defined area will take officers away from other work.[7] We already know that in many other areas investigations of, for instance, individual burglaries are perfunctory, often leading to resentment by victims.[8] While graffiti and the quality of life on the streets are undoubtedly important, most people would feel, I expect, that burglary is a more significant crime.

The arguments for zero tolerance policing are of course based on the 'broken windows' theory – as Roger Hopkins Burke outlined in the first contribution to this volume – which disputes that argument and proposes that by tackling minor incivilities at an early stage it is possible to avert a context in which more serious crime will flourish.[9] It is a very attractive thesis, but the evidence of a causal link between the broken window and serious crime is not yet proven.

In contradiction to the development of zero tolerance we see the development of 'intelligence-led policing'.[10] The theory that underpins this policing strategy assumes that the collection of information and intelligence on criminals rather than 'fire-fighting' each incident is a more efficient and effective use of resources.[11] While I have problems with some of the implications of intelligence-led policing – for example, some of the civil liberties ramifications of certain unsupervised surveillance techniques – effective policing must be the real goal.

Of course, it is not only policing resources that will need to be increased with the implementation of zero tolerance strategies. Every criminal charge will lead to the involvement of the Crown Prosecution Service (CPS), the courts if a prosecution proceeds, defence lawyers with the concurrent provision of legal aid, and finally the probation service. Zero tolerance is also likely to increase the prison population with more, probably inadequate, people sent to prison. It is not inevitable that people who come into contact with the police or other parts of the criminal justice system, for that matter, end up being incarcerated, but there is a real danger that they will. In that case, adoption of the strategy in any general way might overload the penal system completely, causing it to grind to a halt.

Crime on the street

It is extremely likely that zero tolerance policing strategies will be predominately used to target street crime.[12] This raises questions about exactly what is the nature of these offences. I have already briefly mentioned graffiti, and other obvious crimes include begging, spitting, drinking in public, criminal damage, assault and robbery. Some of these are obviously important offences, but in many cases the victim is the local authority or the general public. These particular crimes have significantly less impact on individuals than, say, burglary. Most victims of these more serious offences would be very resistant to the proposal that resources should be directed away from the prevention and investigation of such crimes, because the other offences are trivial and the victim is not an individual.

It may be worth taking action against the first broken window in a particular area as a preventive measure. Nonetheless, we should not automatically concentrate resources to target existing minor social disorder situations. For example, many of us feel unsafe walking through areas with rowdy, noisy drunken youths who are reluctant to observe the usual rules of social etiquette, but I am not convinced that we should devote our precious resources to the eradication of this behaviour. There are, of course, justifications for ensuring that some groups of people, such as women, are safe from assaults, and police and local authorities can do and are doing much to deal with this.[13] My problem is the diversion of limited resources towards the widespread criminalisation of people merely involved in antisocial behaviour, when the emphasis should be on serious crime.

What about more serious crime?

Furthermore, the rigid implementation of zero tolerance-style strategies is contrary to the traditional constitutional provision of the right of the individual police officer to exercise his or her own discretion and to decide which criminal incidents to pursue. In law, this discretion cannot be overridden by the government or the Home Secretary[14] and 'lies at the heart of the policing function'.[15] In fact, Lord Scarman in his 1981 report on the Brixton disorders pointed to the desirability of discretion in policing the streets of the UK.[16]

A police constable's power to act derives not from delegated authority but from 'an original authority'.[17] This confers not only an entitlement for an officer to use his or her legal powers, but also discretion as to how to use them, within the law. Furthermore, the nature of his or her duties obliges the individual officer to exercise discretion. Most decisions must be made without the benefit of supervision, often instantaneously, and sometimes on matters of life and death.[18]

In reality, of course, police discretion can be considered a double-edged sword. Individual police officers may decide to pursue – or not pursue, as the case may be – a course of action against a suspect for highly subjective reasons. Indeed, there are usually vociferous demands for proper management supervision and accountability in such cases.[19]

The discrimination issue

In deciding to adopt zero tolerance policing strategies we are of course making a number of implicit decisions about what is important to us in society. The emphasis on street crime leads inevitably to a concentration on particular kinds of criminal. Crimes on the street are predominately committed by the young, the poor, the unemployed, men, the homeless, the inadequate and those who in the past would have been in institutions.[20] Furthermore, street culture engaged in by certain groups, for instance Afro-Caribbean young men 'hanging out' on the street, the homeless and beggars literally living on the street, makes them a focal point and 'legitimate target' for zero tolerance policing.[21]

There are a number of problems that need to be considered here. The first is whether living on the streets is a criminal problem at all or whether it involves only a clash of different cultures. The second is whether, assuming that the problem exists, the solution should involve the criminalisation of individuals rather than proactive crime prevention strategies of changing the streets by redesign, lighting and improving facilities for those using them. The more radical solution would be to take action to deal with poverty, unemployment, homelessness and the lack of proper community care. Thirdly, there is a great danger that zero tolerance will lead to a further deterioration in relationships between the police, the black community and other marginalised groups. In some areas black and ethnic minority men are twice as likely to be stopped and searched as others.[22] It can be cogently argued that the riots that occurred in the early 1980s were created partly as a result of the zero tolerance of black people on the streets.[23]

Criminalisation

Zero tolerance policing will mean that even larger numbers of people will be dragged through the criminal justice process. For those already alienated from society there is no evidence that it will have a positive effect on their future behaviour. In fact, the experience may make them more antisocial. This is even more likely if the 'crime' is trivial or perceived to be trivial by them. The criminal justice system rarely makes people better. Our legitimate desire to punish should never obscure our ability to concentrate on the outcomes.[24]

What zero tolerance policing will certainly do is to ensure that many people who have no convictions become criminals and those already with a criminal record have more convictions added to it. This matters if we wish to rehabilitate the antisocial person. Already there is considerable prejudice and discrimination against those with criminal records in all areas of life, but particularly in the area of employment.[25]

Recent developments in housing legislation and procedures mean that it will become more difficult for those with criminal convictions to obtain and keep accommodation.[26] The Police Act 1997 provides considerable changes to criminal record vetting. The introduction of Criminal Conviction Certificates is likely to mean that more and more employers will wish to see these before offering employment. Given the number of people unemployed, the amount of discrimination against those with convictions is likely to increase. It is very likely that others will see the 'virtue' of demanding to see certificates before services are provided.

Zero tolerance-style policing will mean, therefore, discrimination against antisocial persons and further exclusions and alienation from society.

Accountability and democracy

Zero tolerance strategies are a clear example of changes being made to the nature of policing which have considerable social and political ramifications without there being any consequential democratic control. Policing policy and the deployment of resources are matters that should be the subject of local democratic control. Previously, Police Authorities were comprised of two-thirds elected representatives, and one-third Justices of the Peace. Subsequent to the Police and Magistrates' Courts Act 1994[27] – which took effect on 1 April 1995 – each Police Authority is a body corporate generally having 17 members, of whom nine will be local councillors and three will be magistrates. Using a shortlist prepared by the Home Secretary, five independent members are selected by a local panel including councillors. There is a real concern that this structure will weaken democratic accountability by reducing the part played by locally elected representatives. Police forces should be accountable to the local community through a democratically elected body. Magistrates and those appointed by the government should not be part of the structures of democracy for the police.

Conclusion

Zero tolerance-style policing carries considerable civil liberties and human rights implications. We must ask ourselves whether we wish to see scarce policing resources diverted

Directed away

from dealing with serious crime to pursuing the perpetrators of petty incivilities and anti-social behaviour. Do we wish to see the targeting of beggars and vandals while the crimes of the powerful such as fraud and corruption go undetected? Zero tolerance policing will inevitably lead to the further expensive criminalisation of the poorer sections of society, with the concordant weakening of their chances of finding legitimate employment and becoming economically independent of the state. In the absence of proper mechanisms of local political accountability for the police service, the question we should be asking is just who is making these decisions to implement zero tolerance policing and in whose interest.

Notes

1   John Wadham is Director of Liberty (formerly the National Council for Civil Liberties), established in 1934. Through the use of a combination of test cases, litigation, research, campaigning and lobbying, Liberty has for over 60 years been protecting civil liberties in the United Kingdom. Liberty's position as one of the leading human rights groups remains unrivalled. It is the largest organisation of its kind in Europe. It is a democratically run membership organisation which is staffed by recognised experts in their field. Committed volunteers also play a key role in the organisation.

  The legal department was set up in 1970 and has established itself as an important source of advice and help for people all over the country who have needed legal advice about their rights. Liberty also conducts test cases in instances where successful litigation will result in public benefits for the protection and extension of human rights and civil liberties in the United Kingdom. Liberty's legal department has considerable expertise in using the European Convention on Human Rights and has more cases pending before the European Commission and Court of Human Rights at any one time than any other lawyer or NGO in this country or in the rest of Europe.

2   See Bratton, W.J. (1997) Crime is Down in New York City: Blame the Police. In Dennis, N. (ed.) *Zero Tolerance: Policing a Free Society*. London: Institute for Economic Affairs.

3   Wilson, J.Q. and Kelling G.L. (1982) Broken Windows. *Atlantic Monthly*, March, pp 29-38; Kelling, G.L. and Coles, C.M. (1996) *Fixing Broken Windows: Restoring Order and Reducing Crime in Our Communities*. New York: The Free Press.

4   The Labour Party (1997) *New Labour Because Britain Deserves Better: Labour Party Manifesto 97*. London: The Labour Party.

5   See Bratton, op cit.

6   See Morgan, R. and Newburn, T. (1997) *The Future of Policing*, Oxford: Clarendon Press for an extensive discussion of the resourcing difficulties facing contemporary police management.

7   See Pollard, C. (1997) Zero Tolerance: Short-term Fix, Long-term Liability. In Dennis, N. (ed.), op cit. In the previous contribution to this volume - 'A Question of Confidence: Zero Tolerance and Problem-Oriented Policing' - Terry Romeanes explains that the Cleveland Constabulary have dealt with this issue through a restructuring of centralised management and

through diverting personnel from the CID to the uniformed branch.

8 See Bayley, D. (1994) *Police for the Future*. New York: Oxford University Press.

9 Wilson and Kelling, op cit.

10 Or 'problem-oriented policing': see Goldstein, H. (1991) *Problem Oriented Policing*. London: McGraw Hill.

11 See Morgan and Newburn, op cit; Pollard, op cit.

12 See Kelling and Coles, op cit; Dennis (ed.), op cit.

13 Research into rates of victimisation has shown that fear of crime may be more justified than criminologists had previously thought. Working-class people living in inner-city areas, experiencing widespread social and economic disadvantage, are far more likely to be the victims of crime than people from other social groups living in different geographical locations. See, for example, Mirlees-Black, C., Mayhew, P. and Percy, A. (1996) *The 1996 British Crime Survey*. Home Office Statistical Bulletin, Issue 19. London: Research and Statistics Directorate.

14 See *R v Metropolitan Police Commissioner, ex parte Blackburn* (No 3) [1973] QB 241; *R v Chief Constable of Devon and Cornwall, ex parte CEGB* [1982] QB 458; and *R v Oxford, ex parte Levey* (1986) *The Times*, 1 November.

15 Scarman, Lord (1981) *The Brixton Disorders 10-12 April 1981: Report of an Inquiry by the Rt Hon. the Lord Scarman, OBE*. London: HMSO, Section 4.58.

16 Ibid.

17 *Fisher* v *Oldham Corporation* [1930] KB 364.

18 Bittner, E. (1970) *The Functions of the Police in Modern Society*. Washington, DC: US Government Printing Office.

19 Regan, D.E. (1983) Are The Police Under Control? *Social Affairs Unit*. 61(1), pp 13-24; Sanders, A. (1993) Controlling the Discretion of the Individual Officer. In Reiner, R. and Spencer, J. (eds) *Accountable Policing*. London: Institute for Public Policy Research.

20 See Taylor, I. (1994) The Political Economy of Crime. In Maguire, M., Morgan, R. and Reiner, R. (eds)*The Oxford Handbook of Criminology*. Oxford: Clarendon Press.

21 See Jerome Miller, cited in Chaudhary, V. and Walker, M. (1996) The Petty Crime War. *The Guardian*, 21 November; Crowther, C. (1997) 'Policing The Excluded Society', in this volume.

22 Keith, M. (1993) *Race, Riots and Policing*. London: UCL Press.

23 See Scarman, op cit; Benyon, J. (ed.) (1984) *Scarman and After*. Oxford: Pergamon.

24 For a full overview of these debates see Morgan, R. (1997) Imprisonment: Current Concerns and a Brief History Since 1945. In Maguire et al (eds), op cit.

25 See, for example, Crow, I., Richardson, P., Riddington, C. and Simon, F. (1989) *Unemployment, Crime and Offenders*. London: RKP; Currie, E. (1985) *Confronting Crime: An American Challenge*. New York: Pantheon; Downes, D. (1993) *Employment Schemes for Offenders*. Home Office, London: HMSO; Evans, R. (1968) The Labour Market and Parole Success. *Journal of Human Resources*. Vol. 3, No. 2, pp 201-12; Farrington, D.P., Gallagher, B., Morley, L., Stledger, R.J. and West, D.J. (1986) Unemployment, School Leaving and Crime. *British Journal of Criminology*. Vol. 26, No. 4, pp 335-56; Lloyd, C., Mair, G. and Hough, M. (1994) *Explaining Reconviction Rates: A Critical Analysis*. Home Office Research Study 133. London: HMSO; Martin, J.P. and Webster, W. (1971) *Social Consequences of Conviction*. London: Heinemann; West, D.J. and Farrington, D. (1977) *The Delinquent Way of Life*. London: Heinemann.

26 The Housing Act 1996 allows possession orders where an arrestable offence has been committed in the dwelling or in its locality.

27 The Police and Magistrates' Courts Act 1994 requires Police Authorities to determine objectives for the policing of the authority's area during the forthcoming financial year; issue a plan setting out the proposed arrangements for the policing of the authority's area for the year; and include in this 'local policing plan' a statement of the authority's priorities for the year, of the resources expected to be available and of the intended allocation of those resources. Morgan and Newburn, op cit, p. 7, observe that:

> The new authorities are to do all this on the advice of their chief constables who are to prepare a draft of the local policing plan for their authorities' consideration. But local policing plans must also take into account national objectives for policing laid down by the Home Secretary. This and other provisions alarmed the police. Sir John Smith, then President of the ACPO (Association of Chief Police Officers), took the view that 'we are witnessing a move, perhaps unintended, for national control of the police by central government'.

Chapter 5

Below Zero Tolerance: The New York Experience

Eli B. Silverman[1]

Introduction

At the time of my first visit to the UK in 1984 – as the visiting Bramshill exchange professor[2] – the hot topic in policing, the flavour of the month, was an idea imported from the USA, 'Policing by Objectives'. The emphasis was on 'value for money' and measurement of that value through the application to the police of management techniques borrowed largely from the world of business.[3] The current fashion in UK policing is another importation from the USA,[4] the inaccurately termed 'zero tolerance'.[5] It is the purpose of this paper to explore what I understand to be some UK reservations concerning the New York City model of that form of policing.

Six zero tolerance myths

The approach of this paper will be to address some common myths surrounding the issue of zero tolerance policing in New York City.

Myth number one: 'zero tolerance is fundamentally counter to policing by consent. The focus is on repression by enforcement'[6]

According to former Chief Superintendent Caroline Nicholl of the Thames Valley Police, whose views are summarised in this quote, zero tolerance policing violates the wishes of the community and the police come to be seen as a kind of alien occupation army. This it is argued, is especially true in the poor and ethnic minority communities.

I propose that anyone holding such views visit the poorest ethnic minority communities in New York City, where they will find that the residents are considerably more satisfied with the police service and the results it has achieved than before the implementation of the so-called 'zero tolerance' policing revolution. Admittedly, satisfaction levels are not as high as they are in the middle-class white communities, where incidentally the major complaint is that the poorer communities are getting more police than they are them-

selves. They are, however, substantially higher than before.[7] This is not to say that alienation may not happen and that we should not be constantly on the lookout for it. But to date
it has not occurred. Most members of the community who have previously been victims
welcome the decline in crime when the police are attentive to their rights.

It is important to note that the community also has rights. Successful zero tolerance policing is more in harmony with community wishes than is the abandonment of public spaces
to those who violate other people's rights, privacy and passage.[8] I am aware that Sir
Robert Peel stressed policing by consent.[9] The evidence of New York City nonetheless
demonstrates widespread consent for zero tolerance-style policing and the citizenry do
not wish to be denied.[10]

*Myth number two: zero tolerance policing controls crime by essentially segregating the
underclass*

Many of the so-called underclass are themselves the victims of crime. It is these very
groups who have experienced the most dramatic decline in crimes and who have also
welcomed the police presence in their communities. One UK author notes that the importation of US zero tolerance policing styles would result in:

> sweeping clear those inner city junctions whose tourists and professional commut-
> ers briefly encounter the dispossessed underclass – the mad and sad, as well as the
> bad. ... So-called zero tolerance policing is actually discriminatory intolerance of
> vulnerable nuisance groups operating in symbolic locations.[11]

He then goes on to note that:

> This observation fits in a well documented tradition of the selective and discretion-
> ary policing of various marginalised and minority groups.[12]

Contrary to this assertion, the New York City communities with the most persistent decline in crime since 1993 are scarcely visited by tourists. The beneficiaries reside in the
boroughs of Brooklyn and the Bronx and are among the poorest and least skilled citizens.
These areas are now experiencing an economic revival. While one may choose not to
believe that the police have contributed to this , I believe that they have.

Myth number three: zero tolerance policing is just about enforcement

Charles Pollard, Chief Constable of Thames Valley Police, has notably articulated this
view:

> Zero tolerance in New York suggests tackling low-level disorder and incivilities,
> albeit through a narrow, aggressive and uncompromising law enforcement approach.[13]

Former Thames Valley Chief Superintendent Caroline Nicholl observed that:

> (Police) Performance in New York is now entirely measured in numerical terms of arrests, search warrants, tickets, etc.[14]

I do not know the Chief Superintendent, but I do strongly disagree with her. The main measure of performance in New York is the crime rate. If a precinct's arrests, search warrants, tickets, etc have increased and the crime rate is still up, they need to do something differently. What is more, they do not have to be told that. They are fully aware that these conditions will emerge at a CompStat crime strategy meeting – see Roger Hopkins Burke, 'A Contextualisation of Zero Tolerance Policing Strategies', in this volume – if they forget this lesson. Results are more important than activities. It is not that activities are unimportant. It is that their importance lies in their relationship to crime results.

The New York Police Department (NYPD) has devised an informational base and process (known as CompStat) that provides both the data and the setting for consistently comparing results with activities, means with ends, arrests with crime reduction, quality of life summons with index crime, deployment strategies with crime results, etc. It is this CompStat process that constitutes the substructure that supports the various strategic approaches of which zero tolerance is just one. I believe that these organisational and management innovations are the most important changes in the New York policing revolution – hence the title of this paper, 'Below Zero Tolerance'.

Furthermore, the notion that there is a connection between fear of crime, disorder and crime is no longer just an hypothesis as some still claim. The studies and examples are legion. One 60-day pilot study of illegal car window washers – 'squeegees' we call them, a central target of zero tolerance-style policing strategies in New York City[15] – revealed that 50% had previous arrests for serious felonies and 50% had previous convictions for drug-related offences.[16]

The key lies less in arrests *per se* than it does in public contact. Much of this contact is in the form of summons activity with such elements as marijuana smoking, disorderly conduct, contravening parking regulations, public urination, public drinking, bicycle offences, windshield washing, alcohol beverage control, no certificates of authenticity, possession of a knife over four inches. A summons, nonetheless, is only issued if the individual possesses a government-issued photo identification and there are no active warrants out for their arrest. Otherwise they are arrested, debriefed and taken off the streets (and therefore not committing crimes).

For example, take the seemingly innocuous riding of bicycles, which lately have been used to facilitate robberies, shootings and drug transactions. One commanding officer identified laws regulating the operation of bicycles. Enforcement began and by the end of summer 1996 success resulted in nineteen guns being found from this source in just one precinct. This success was heralded at a CompStat meeting and resulted in a city-wide adoption of this strategy. It has subsequently yielded hundreds of guns and large quantities of narcotics taken off these previously invisible people on bicycles. Again, locations and times are targeted for specific reasons.

In one of the most crime-ridden precincts, to take another example, the quality of life violation summons total increased from 569 in 1993 to 4933 in 1996 – an increase of over 767%. In the same period the overall decrease in 'seven index crimes' (serious felonies) was from 10,355 in 1993 to 6,814 in 1996.[17] In short, targeting and apprehending minor offenders has substantially reduced their opportunity to become involved in more serious offences.

Myth number four: zero tolerance is anti- or non-responsive to the community

Should there be a partnership with the communities? Of course. Is there police community interaction in New York City? Yes. As a group, precinct commanders and their staff are more in contact with the communities today than at any time during the past ten years. They are now in a position to be more sensitive to community needs because along with zero tolerance-style policing, precinct commanders have more authority, as well as accountability, than they ever had before. This is a part of the organisational and managerial changes to which I have previously referred.

The emphasis on quality of life enforcement is much more in harmony with the wishes of the community than just major crime enforcement. In our country, it is the quality of life offences that most trouble citizens – the violations of human civility that allow communities to fall into disrepair. Survey after survey in place after place has demonstrated this.[18] For about a year, the NYPD has instituted a telephone hotline for citizens to complain about quality of life – non-major – offences. What do you think the major complaint is – repeatedly, week after week, month after month? It is noise. This may be surprising to us, but it should not be.[19]

The more successful zero tolerance-style initiatives are those that consult with the community beforehand and heed their concerns. They are not inherently incompatible. For example, in New York, the number of police-public interactions increased substantially in 1996. Although the percentage of arrests increased by only 1.28%, total interaction increased at much higher percentages. Parking summonses increased by over 7%, moving summonses by just under 5%, and criminal summonses, the majority of the so-called quality of life offences, by just under 30%. Despite this increase, citizens' complaints have slightly declined.[20]

Should the police always strive for more partnership with the community? Of course. But the point is that the concepts of community involvement and zero tolerance are not diametrically opposed.

Myth number five: zero tolerance leaves the police no discretion

Nothing could be further from the truth. Zero tolerance does not mean 24 hours a day, 7 days a week, perpetual enforcement of all quality of life offences. It does mean selective enforcement, as part of overall strategies, targeted to specific problems, whether it relates to drugs, guns, youth social clubs, etc. Strategies may include a vast array of tactics, including car searches, warrant checks and a range of community and social agency involvement. All, however, are directed to a particular problem, based on their geographic and temporal crime distribution, which we know generally falls into clusters. These approaches often include team-led enforcement operations which entail co-ordinated plans of action with transit and housing divisions, special posts, observation posts, plainclothes, narcotics teams, sting operations and intensive debriefing by detectives. Today, police forces are far more focused on integrating the generalist beat officers with the specialist units.

Zero tolerance is not practised everywhere all the time. Even if there were sufficient resources to do so, and as the critics rightly note there are not, that is not the objective. The real question is not zero tolerance policing: it is smarter policing, as I believe you are also experiencing in the UK.

Myth number six: zero tolerance is anti-problem solving

This strikes me as part of a larger theme I have encountered, that somehow zero tolerance-style policing is intolerant of other policing approaches. The Thames Valley Chief Constable, Charles Pollard, is quoted in the *Police Review* as saying:

> Zero tolerance implies that there is just one solution – tougher policing – for all crime problems.[21]

I do not know how or why this is true. There is nothing I know about zero tolerance-style policing that is inherently incompatible with simultaneously addressing short-run problems and long-range solutions. In America, there is a federal funding programme in which the police, in conjunction with local governments and social agencies address specific community programmes. It is known as 'weed and seed'. As the name implies, one needs to aggressively weed out the outgrowth before one cultivates long-term growth.

Some precincts with the most intensive and directed policing also have key programmes in which community activists are involved in the design, implementation and the spending of government funds. As a matter of fact, I believe there is more systematic problem solving going on in the NYPD than ever before, for example, the closing down of store fronts involved in illegal activities such as gambling or narcotics - called nuisance abatement – through civil enforcement. This approach works by permitting the NYPD to sue landlords renting their premises to criminals who use them for these purposes. It requires documentation of three incidents of criminal activity, usually obtained by undercover police work, and this is forwarded to the Civil Enforcement Unit attorneys who prepare cases and bring them to court. The judge subsequently signs an order closing the location for one year unless a legitimate tenant is found and approved by the attorneys. This policy reduces public perceptions of revolving-door justice that had previously occurred following criminal convictions where offenders would leave court and recommence their activities in the same premises shortly afterwards. Furthermore, there is a substantial reduction in the shootings, robberies and other crimes which surround these core problem locations.

Furthermore, CompStat, with its collation and collection of information, has developed as an instrument to reveal, demonstrate and revise these problem-solving approaches among precincts. For example, a city-wide strategy of closing down 'chop shops' to cut down on the number of motor vehicle thefts arose out of one precinct with an officer who at the time was a member of the community policing unit. Operation 'Close Out', another example, was created and implemented by one precinct's community policing unit in order to target suspected narcotic sales locations for immediate closure. The specifically trained team utilise laws not normally enforced by uniformed patrol officers, for example, by ascertaining whether premises have acquired a valid certificate of doing business. This general business law is then used to gain entry and review the activities of commercial premises.

Conclusion

How does one account for the currency of the myths? In addition to definitional issues, perhaps the reservations about zero tolerance-style policing primarily stem from disparate theories on crime causation and the impact that the police can have on crime.

It appears that the sceptics favour criminological theories that emphasise social and economic inequality and the impact of the market economy.[22] This is surely a respectable position. This view stresses prevailing social, economic and demographic conditions as placing major constraints upon likely successful police activity. The list is unending: unemployment, drug markets and drug dealings, poverty, overcrowding, public housing, incarceration rates, death rates, youth demographics. One researcher has recently asserted that crime rates in large cities can be predicted accurately 80 to 90 per cent of the time when one takes into account such economic and social factors as income, unemployment, education, prevalence of minorities, households headed by single women, household size and home ownership.[23]

Other scholars have indirectly confirmed these views. For too long, The Kansas City Preventive Patrol Experiment[24] and other studies, for example, led many to fallaciously conclude that there were ironclad constraints on police effectiveness. As recently as 1990, two widely read and highly influential criminologists, Gottfredson and Hirschi, observed that:

> no evidence exists that augmentation of police forces or equipment, differential patrol strategies, or differential intensities of surveillance have an effect on crime rates.[25]

Moreover, police were warned by liberal commentators and criminologists not to take credit for declining crime rates since they would be blamed for the inevitable rise in crime.[26] We have some evidence of self-imposed restraints.

It was a defeatist view of policing, however, that had failed to recognise or acknowledge the possibilities offered by situational crime prevention to address a whole range of issues related to opportunities, victims, the nature and patterns of times, places and choices.[27] An approach which allows, I believe, for greater policing impacts. Recently, more criminologists have backed off from the failed grand theoretical designs of the past and have been converted to the more down-to-earth pragmatic situational approach. As an editor of a scholarly journal recently wrote:

> Over the last two decades, criminologists have had an attack of conscience. Humbled by past theoretical mistakes, some major and others simply naive, we are properly wary of imposing our limited insights on the world.[28]

Consequently, we should focus on the most important issues and lessons to have emerged from the New York police experience and more recent literature on policing activities and results. The central issues of common concern to have emerged are as follows:

- *Targeted police activities.* It is important to reflect on exactly what type of police presence and targeted activities impact on what types of crime. We need to think about how selected and focused police activities impact on what some criminologists call the lack of randomness of crime in time and space and the convergence in space and time of motivated offenders, suitable targets, and the absence of capable guardians.[29]

- *Drugs and crimes.* It is necessary to consider the possible connections between drug misuse and other crime and how the police can have an impact on this relationship.

- *Drug market analysis.* We should heed the role of drug market analysis in defining and focusing on high-incidence drug crime areas.

- *Hot spot analyses.* It is important to reflect on the impacts of various hot spot analyses of criminal activity and the concordant deployment of police. It is necessary to contemplate optimal concentrations of law enforcement and other organised resources.

- *Quality of life enforcement.* It is important to study the role of quality of life enforcement and other police/public interactions, not just arrests – for too long we have been wedded to major crimes and their concomitant arrests and impacts. Police practice and research have clearly demonstrated that major crimes cannot be viewed as the only significant variables to be examined.

- *Dampening disorder.* We have to think about how selected targeted police activities dampen disorder. In other words, we need to consider the extent and degree to which police activities increase the certainty of detection and apprehension.

- *Preventable crime.* It is necessary to contemplate the different types of preventable crime, for example, domestic violence, and then consider appropriate preventive strategies.

- *Displacement.* We need to consider the conditions under which displacement does follow or does not follow police intervention. We must reflect on the actual level of displacement and exactly where it goes. How much of it goes to areas where there is less serious crime or days of the week or periods of time when there are fewer potential victims? In this case we must ask ourselves whether displacement offers a diffusion of benefits.[30]

- *Community involvement.* Finally, we need to consider the nature of the reciprocal interactions and impacts between the police and community involvement. We need to take into account how one stimulates the other in crime reduction.[31]

In essence, what I believe zero tolerance strategies are ultimately about is refusing to accept the notion that the police cannot seriously impact upon crime. There is zero tolerance for resignation to rising crime rates. Operations are assessed from ground zero. It is akin to what organisational theorists call double-loop learning. This contrasts with single-loop learning, the predominant mode of most organisations, which occurs when the detection and correction of error enables the organisation to continue with its present policies or achieve its present objectives. Double-loop learning, on the other hand, is rarer and more fundamental since it involves questioning basic operating assumptions, entertaining disparate approaches and experimenting with various arrangements.[32]

This is not only smarter policing, it is far more difficult policing, since it involves less standardised and more flexible hours, assignments, and greater mobility in your force. It means more up-to-date information, consistent crime analysis and relentless focused attention to problems. As such, it is also more demanding upon the police organisations – and consequently there is bound to be organisational resistance. Commitment and dedication are prerequisites for effective policing, whatever the label.

Notes

1   Eli B. Silverman is Professor of Police Science at John Jay College of Criminal Justice in New York City and for two years headed a research project investigating the policing revolution instigated in that city by the former Police Commissioner, William J. Bratton. Dr Silverman is also the author of a forthcoming book on the New York City Police Department and Compstat.

Founded in 1964, John Jay College of Criminal Justice of The City University of New York is a liberal arts college which emphasises as its special mission criminal justice, fire science, and other public service-related fields. As such, it is the only one of its kind in the nation.

The College serves as a major centre for research in criminal justice, law enforcement, and forensic sciences, and as a major training facility for local, state, federal and international law enforcement agencies, and private security personnel.

Its ethnically and culturally diverse student population, in excess of 9,500, includes 25 per cent who are members of the uniformed criminal justice and fire service agencies. The majority of the students are civilian pre-professionals who plan careers in public service or are already employed in public service.

The College hosts major conferences attracting national and world leaders to discuss crime, drug abuse and violence, and to develop meaningful solutions to these problems.

2   As part of the United Kingdom's National Police Training, the Police Staff College, Bramshill, is the principal seat of learning for current and future police leaders, and is responsible for delivering a comprehensive programme of higher training, including international police training.

Bramshill is known worldwide as a centre of excellence in the training and development of senior police officers. Since 1970 its international reputation has been particularly enhanced by the attendance of more than 1,000 high-ranking police officers from over 83 countries on overseas command courses.

3   For a full discussion, see Morgan, R. and Newburn, T. (1997) *The Future of Policing*. Oxford: Clarendon Press.

4   Fashions change. This is not surprising. What I fail to comprehend, however, is how the two cultures shift and spread back and forth, to and from both sides of the Atlantic. For some reason, we seem to mimic British Andrew Lloyd Webber theatre, pop music, fashions and novels, and you seem to reverse the process with our movies, novels and trends in policing. I am not sure who gets the better of the deal. Although with the exchange of television programmes, I believe the Americans profit.

5   The phrase itself is best conceived as a container concept that incorporates a range of different policing strategies that are introduced and periodically adjusted. Perhaps another title for my paper could be 'Zeroing in on Zero Tolerance'.

6   Chief Superintendent Caroline Nicholl, Minutes of 'Zero Tolerance Conference', Henry Fielding Centre, University of Manchester, 24 March 1997. Manchester: University of Manchester.

7   This view is substantiated by Kelling, G.L. and Coles, C.M. (1996) *Fixing Broken Windows: Restoring Order and Reducing Crime in Our Communities*. New York: The Free Press.

8   See ibid, where this view is also positively reinforced.

9   Sir Robert Peel became Home Secretary of the UK in 1828. He recognised from the outset the importance of establishing a new police service in the country with the primary role of preventing crime and disorder rather than being a reactive organisation dependent upon detecting incidents after they had occurred. He was also conscious of the failings of the contemporary social control procedures, the fears of many individuals about the corrupt practices of those involved in the process, and the loss of civil liberties that would arise with a new professionalised police force. Peel established a full-time paid police force but considered that the rest of the population should police their own communities on a part-time basis as they went about their day-to-day activities. See Critchley, T.A. (1978) *A History of the Police in England and Wales*. London: Constable.

10 Roger Hopkins Burke provides further support for this view in his contribution to this volume - 'A Contextualisation of Zero Tolerance Policing Strategies' - where he shows that the Mayor of New York City, Rudolph Giuliani, who is widely associated with the implementation of this approach to policing, has bucked electoral trends in the city and become extremely popular.

11 Morgan, R. (1997) Law and Order: Swept Along by Zero Option. *The Guardian*, 22 January, p 22.

12 Ibid.

13 Pollard, C. (1997) Zero Tolerance: Short-term Fix, Long-term Liability. In Dennis, N. (ed.) *Zero Tolerance: Policing a Free Society*. London: Institute for Economic Affairs, p 44.

14 Nicholl, op cit. See also her remarks in *Police Review*, 4 April 1997, p 17.

15 See Kelling and Coles, op cit.

16 Lynch, C. (1993) War on Windshield Washers. *The Boston Globe*, 18 December, p 3.

17 NYPD Statistics - Field Notes (unpublished).

18 For a full overview, see Kelling and Coles, op cit.

19 A similar situation exists in the UK where studies have shown that the public feel that the police service should spend more time investigating offences such as fighting/rowdyism in the streets, parking/traffic offences and litter than it does on crimes such as sexual assaults on women, residential burglary and drunken driving. See Joint Consultative Committee of the Police Staff Associations of England and Wales (1990) *Operational Policing Review*. Surbiton: Joint Consultative Committee.

20 NYPD Statistics - Field Notes (unpublished).

21 Chief Constable Charles Pollard, quoted in *Police Review*, 4 April 1997, p 17.

22 See the paper - 'Policing the Excluded Society' - by Dr Chris Crowther in this volume, which provides an overview of that position.

23 Bayley, D. (1996) Measuring Overall Effectiveness. In Hoover, L.T. (ed.) *Quantifying Quality in Policing*. Washington DC: Police Executive Research Forum, p 41.

24 Kelling, G.L., Pate, T., Dieckman, D. and Brown, C. (1974) *The Kansas City Preventive Patrol Experiment: A Summary Report*. Washington, DC: The Police Foundation. Results of this study showed that substantial changes in levels of preventive patrol had no impact on levels of crime or citizen perceptions about the safety of neighbourhoods.

25 Gottfredson, M. and Hirschi, T. (1990) *A General Theory of Crime*. Stanford: Stanford University Press, p 270.

26 For a full overview, see Kelling and Coles, op cit; see also Bratton, W.J. (1997) Crime is Down in New York City: Blame the Police. In Dennis, N. (ed.), op cit.

27 See, for example, Clarke, R.V.G. (1980) Situational Crime Prevention: Theory and Practice. In Muncie, J., McLaughlin, E. and Langan, M. (eds) (1996) *Criminological Perspectives: A Reader*. London: Sage; Brantingham, P.J. and Brantingham, P.L. (eds) (1981) *Environmental Criminology*. Beverly Hills: Sage; Reiss, A.J. and Tonry, M. (eds) (1986) *Communities and Crime*. Chicago: University of Chicago Press; Walklate, S. (1992) Appreciating the Victim: Conventional,

Realist or Critical Victimology? In Matthews, R. and Young, J. (eds) *Issues in Realist Criminology*. London: Sage; Felson, M. (1994) *Crime and Everyday Life*. Thousand Oaks, CA: Pine Forge.

28 Erez, E. (1995) From the Editor. *Justice Quarterly*. Vol. 12, No. 4, December, p 619.

29 See, for example, Felson, op cit.

30 See Clarke, op cit; Clarke, R.V.G. (1991) Deterring Obscene Phone Callers: The New Jersey Experience. In Clarke, R.V.G. (ed.) *Situational Crime Prevention: Successful Case Studies*. New York: Harrow and Heston; Clarke, R.V.G. and Cornish, D. (1985) Modelling Offenders' Decisions: A Framework for Policy and Research. In Morris, N. and Tonry, M. (eds) *Crime and Justice, An Annual Review of Research*. Vol. 6. Chicago: University of Chicago Press; Clarke, R.V.G., Field, S. and McGrath, G. (1991) Target Hardening of Banks in Australia and Displacement of Robberies. *Security Journal*. Vol. 2, pp 84-90; Clarke, R.V.G. and Mayhew, P.M. (1988) The British Gas Suicide Story and its Criminological Implications. In Morris, N. and Tonry, M. (eds) *Crime and Justice: An Annual Review of Research*. Vol 10. Chicago: Chicago University Press; Cornish, D. and Clarke, R.V.G. (1986) *The Reasoning Criminal: Rational Choice Perspectives on Offending*. New York: Springer-Verlag; Cornish, D. and Clarke, R.V.G. (1988a) Understanding Crime Displacement: An Application of Rational Choice Theory. *Criminology*. Vol. 7, pp 933-47; Cornish, D. and Clarke, R.V.G. (1988b) Crime Specialisation, Crime Displacement and Rational Choice Theory. In Wegener, H. Losel, F. and Haisch, J. (eds) *Criminal Behaviour and the Justice System: Psychological Perspectives*. New York: Springer-Verlag.

31 See Morgan and Newburn, op cit; Reiner, R. (1997) Policing and the Police. In Maguire, M., Morgan, R. and Reiner, R. (eds) *The Oxford Handbook of Criminology*. Oxford: Clarendon Press; Smith, D. (1987) The Police and the Idea of Community. In Wilmott, P. (ed.) *Policing and the Community*. London: Policy Studies Institute.

32 Argyris, C. (1982) *Reasoning, Learning and Action*. San Francisco: Josey Bass; Argyris, C. (1990) *Overcoming Organisational Defences: Facilitating Organisational Learning*. Needham Heights, Mass: Allyn and Bacon.

Chapter 6

Policing The Excluded Society

Chris Crowther[1]

Introduction

The notion of 'zero tolerance' policing has had a profound impact on recent political and public debate about social exclusion, crime and disorder. At the same time there has been considerable disagreement both in the USA and UK about whether or not it is an effective method of tackling certain types of offending behaviour. In the UK it has won the support of the main political parties, although certain influential senior police officers do not share the same level of enthusiasm.[2]

This paper examines some of the different ideas about zero tolerance policing in the context of a wider discussion of contemporary policing styles. There is a particular focus on the contention of Robert Reiner that since the birth of the modern police force in 1829 the 'main grist of the mill of routine policing ... [has been] the "underclass"'.[3] The main aim is to examine the concept of zero tolerance in the context of Reiner's thesis. First, there is an assessment of the extent to which this style of policing links in with routine police activity. Second, there is a critical examination of the relationship between this approach to policing and the so-called 'underclass'.

Zero tolerance shares some common traits with traditional patterns of policing. Since 1829 the prevention/detection of crime and the preservation of public tranquillity - especially the latter - have been the core tasks of the police service. However, in recent times, successive UK governments have questioned some of the assumptions on which the modern police were founded. In addition, the conventional wisdom of academic and police opinion, that solutions to the twin problems of crime and disorder ultimately lie beyond the police,[4] has been challenged. This has resulted in fundamental change to the day-to-day operations of the organisation. According to government policy, keeping the Queen's peace should take second place to enforcing the law and catching criminals. This transformation has been driven by reforms which require the police to demonstrate that they are economic, efficient and, most importantly, effective. Zero tolerance is such an example.

The first task is to define the term the 'underclass' and examine different explanations for its apparent existence. Second, there is a consideration of the relationship between zero tolerance and traditional models of policing. Third, there is a brief review of the key trends in zero tolerance policing in the UK and the USA. Finally, there is a discussion of the view that zero tolerance is primarily directed against the so-called 'underclass', which is made up of excluded groups such as the homeless and beggars[5] and/or the 'rough working class'.[6] I will proceed by examining what is meant by the term the 'underclass'.

Perspectives on the 'underclass'

There are primarily two academic perspectives on the 'underclass', the behavioural and the structural.[7] Structural accounts are normally associated with the political 'left' and are primarily concerned with highlighting various forms of social exclusion, poverty, material deprivation and patterns of inequality.[8] For structuralists, the inadequacy of state-provided welfare services, changes in the labour market and exclusion from full citizenship are the main factors leading to the emergence of an 'underclass'.

The behavioural perspective is normally associated with the political 'right' and came to prominence during the 1980s with the rise in the number of long-term unemployed, the burgeoning lone-parent population, increased welfare dependency, and rising crime and disorder.[9] Behaviourists focus on the damaging effects of state-provided social services on the character and behaviour of individuals.[10] They argue that state welfare erodes individual responsibility by giving people incentives not to work and provide for themselves and their family, thereby creating dependency on state services. Moreover, it is argued that the 'controls' which stop individuals and communities from behaving badly, such as stable family backgrounds and, in particular, positive male role models, do not exist for some, most notably members of the 'underclass'.

Sociological research studies have seriously challenged the view that non-participation in the labour market contributes, in any simple way, to the creation of a distinctive subculture.[11] Other academics have observed that these studies cannot account for the real problems of crime and antisocial behaviour that plague some local communities.[12] They recognise that care should be taken not to blame the poor for their own condition but at the same time find it difficult to justify some of their actions, particularly those which victimise other vulnerable individuals. It is therefore necessary to address activities such as undeclared work, thieving and begging, and these antisocial elements are, for the proponents of this perspective, a legitimate target for police intervention.

Let us now consider the veracity of Reiner's argument cited above, namely that the bulk of police activity is oriented towards an 'underclass'. I do this by considering some models of policing intervention in the contemporary UK.

Policing: the same old debates or new directions?

Distinguishing new patterns of policing from what has gone before is not always clear-cut. Certainly, since its inception the police service has been constantly responsible for performing the two core tasks noted in the introduction. Performing these sometimes

conflicting and incompatible roles has led to what Lord Scarman referred to as 'the policing dilemma.'[13] Throughout the history of the police service one of these goals has been
achieved at the expense of the other.[14] Following the unrest in the inner cities of the UK in
the 1980s and the publication of the Scarman Report into the Brixton disorders, the 'preservation of the Queen's peace' became the top policing priority. More recently, crime-
fighting has taken precedence. Indeed, the concept of 'keeping the peace' receives no
mention in recent reform documents.[15] It is precisely this concern that some senior officers have raised regarding the introduction of zero tolerance policing strategies. Charles
Pollard, Chief Constable of Thames Valley Police, is anxious that zero tolerance may
recreate the problems found in urban areas in the 1980s when the prioritisation of 'crime-
fighting' criteria compromised the attempts of the police service to maintain public order.
Pollard also maintains that this approach is contrary to the key principles of community
policing, especially a version called 'problem-oriented policing'.[16] I will return to this
issue later in this paper.

The recent transition in the nature of policing mentioned above, including the introduction of zero tolerance, has taken place in the context of rapid social, economic, political
and ideological change. Innovations in police policy and practice must therefore be situ-
ated in relation to these broad developments in the political economy, particularly central
government policy.[17]

In the early 1980s the police were Baroness Thatcher's 'boys in blue'[18] and the key agency
in the fight against crime and the various political 'enemies within'. It was a situation that
did not last for long, and the disciplines of the market were gradually applied to the
service. Kenneth Clarke's NHS reforms, launched in 1989, later became the model on
which these fundamental reforms were based. During his period as Home Secretary the
police rapidly declined in popularity in government circles because, despite the investment of more and more resources, crime rates continued to increase inexorably. As noted
in the introduction, one of the old shibboleths of liberal criminology subsequently came
under attack. The view that remedies to the problems of crime and disorder are beyond
the responsibility of the police was questioned. Rather, they found themselves in a position of needing to justify their existence by providing a value-for-money service.

Three central 'reforms' were introduced to achieve this end, and each has had significant
consequences for the police service. First, the identification of separate 'core' and 'ancil-
lary' functions has led to a fundamental reassessment of its organisational structure and
culture.[19] Second, the introduction of 'new public management' and market disciplines
has led to the contracting out of tasks to the private sector.[20] Third, 'performance indicators' have been established by the Home Office which, by and large, measure performance on the basis of 'crime-fighting' criteria.[21] However, there has also been a trend towards decentralisation with an enhanced role for police authorities – in principle, if not in
practice – in formulating 'local policing plans'.[22] The first three reforms were ill-suited to
the community policing model that had been dominant since the Scarman Report[23] and
which did not easily lend itself to quantifiable outcomes. John Alderson (Chief Constable
of Devon and Cornwall Police 1973-82) had detailed the philosophy of community or
communitarian policing[24] that was later incorporated into the recommendations of the

Scarman Report.[25] It was specifically designed to prevent and detect crime while maintaining public order, especially amongst a socially excluded 'underclass'. These founding goals are still in place, but there have been other developments which will be acknowledged in due course.

Community policing consists of three dimensions. First, there is a need for the physical presence of officers in particular areas. Second, police-community consultative committees were established by statute[26] to provide an institutionalised forum to discuss local policing policy and practice. Third, there is the encouragement of inter-agency or multi-agency co-operation with the intention of restoring social cohesion to communities with high levels of social exclusion. It is the rationale of this approach that decision-making is decentralised and more democratic. Plans and policy are developed through community consultation and public co-operation, with the aim of improving relations between the police and community. This is considered necessary for the maintenance of public order. It will be shown that zero tolerance includes all these elements as well as some further novel ones.

The Home Office came to question the value of a communitarian model which proposes that the modern police service is primarily a peace-keeping organisation rather than a crime-fighting force. Consequently, the introduction of reforms based on the disciplines of the market – efficiency, economy and effectiveness – has led to different demands being made of the police, with performance now measured in terms of ability to clear up crime.[27] The wisdom of this change of emphasis has, however, been challenged by senior police officers,[28] and in 1994 John Hoddinott – Chief Constable of Hampshire and former President of ACPO[29] – wrote that:

> there were circumstances where enforcement of the law had, of necessity, to be accorded a lesser priority than the maintenance of order.[30]

Significantly, zero tolerance policing strategies have been focused on incivilities and low-level disorder as part of an attempt to reduce crime. The two phenomena are considered related. I have argued that the relationship between them is far from clear-cut, and that policing has traditionally been about recognising the differences between them. There is the danger that the need for different responses to crime and disorder respectively may be overlooked.

At this stage, it is necessary to put zero tolerance into context. Debates in police and government circles which preceded the decision to adopt these strategies were justified on the basis of what happened in the USA. Let us now consider some examples of the supposed success of zero tolerance which informed debates in the UK, particularly journalistic accounts. The links between this strategy and the 'underclass' are also teased out.

Some recent debates about 'zero tolerance'

The 'zero tolerance' policing strategy introduced by William J. Bratton in New York City has apparently been extremely successful. Since the introduction of the scheme in the summer of 1994 the number of homicides has decreased from 1,582 to 1,182 in 1995 and 983 in 1996. In 1990 the figure was 2,245, thus indicating that the rate was falling anyway. For robbery, in 1993 there were 85,892 recorded offences, compared to 59,721 a year after the strategy was launched.[31] These statistics should be treated with caution, however, because there are other possible factors that help explain such a reduction, including: a displacement effect; demographic changes, particularly a decline in the youth population; increased job opportunities following the end of an especially bad period of recession; and the introduction of more mandatory and longer prison sentences which have resulted in 'criminals' being kept off the streets for longer periods. It is therefore difficult to isolate the effects of zero tolerance policing on crime and disorder.[32] In the UK, evidence has also been marshalled to justify this mode of policing.

On 18 November 1996 the Metropolitan Police implemented a six-week experiment, 'Operation Zero Tolerance', in collaboration with the City of London Police and the British Transport Police, in King's Cross. The experiment was built on 'Operation Welwyn', also initiated by the Metropolitan Police, in co-operation with Islington and Camden Councils, in 1992. The purpose of this partnership between the police, public sector, private and voluntary agencies, as well as the general public, was:

> to target and prevent crimes which are a particular local problem, including drug-related criminality.[33]

Significantly, since the introduction of 'Operation Zero Tolerance' politicians and police in the UK have targeted particular groups in 'underclass'-type positions, such as beggars and the homeless. The rationale for this approach is outlined in a Home Office report submitted to Ministers which stated that:

> anti-social behaviour can stimulate criminality by creating an environment that attracts the more criminally inclined and implies that their conduct will not be subjected to effective controls.[34]

'Operation Zero Tolerance' included elements of Bratton's approach of targeting minor crimes such as dropping litter, graffiti, aggressive begging, and low-level disorder,[35] adapted to deal with specific problems found in some locales in London, combined with pre-existing initiatives such as 'partnership policing'.[36] There have certainly been successes.

Evaluations of 'Operation Welwyn' show that since 1992 425 drug dealers have been convicted, and it is estimated that the number of street drug dealers operating in the area has also fallen. Moreover, initial appraisals suggest that there has been an improvement in the quality of life of residents and workers in the targeted areas.[37]

Hartlepool and Middlesbrough, in Cleveland, are two of the few places – outside of London – where a police force has explicitly used zero tolerance-style policing.[38] Since the strategy was adopted in Hartlepool the number of recorded offences has been halved. In Middlesbrough reported crime was reduced by one–fifth within six weeks. Before Christmas 1996 an average of 75 crimes (20 of these were burglaries) were committed each day. By February 1997 the comparable figures were 60 and 12 respectively.[39]

A similar scheme - 'Spotlight Initiative'[40] - piloted by Strathclyde Police in Glasgow commenced on 1 October 1996. After consulting the public, the police found that people were substantially more anxious about the security of their property and their personal safety in public places than they were about the possibility of becoming victims of serious crimes such as murder and rape. In partnership with Customs and Excise and local authorities they devoted a significant proportion of their operational resources to target all crimes by implementing 20,000 stop and searches in the first month. Overall, the number of recorded offences fell by 9%. Drug related arrests rose by 1,300. Serious assaults declined by 12%, robberies by 5%, common assaults by 4% and break-ins by 9%. Recorded incidents of arson fell by 10%, vandalism by 4% and there were 1,687 fewer crimes against motor vehicles.[41]

Although zero tolerance is far from being an homogeneous style of policing, there are some themes common to each of the above schemes. Furthermore, there are some striking parallels between these and Alderson's model of community policing, mentioned earlier on. First, they all rely heavily on a visible presence of police officers. Second, all the schemes have been introduced in response to public anxiety about high levels of crime and disorder and more general concerns about community safety. Third, there is an emphasis on the police consulting different public, private and voluntary agencies. Indeed, the forthcoming Crime and Disorder Bill will place a statutory responsibility on local authorities to work with the police to tackle crime and disorder and to set local targets for reducing the scale and prevalence of these social problems. As Home Office Minister Alun Michael recently announced:

> What we will do is place a new joint responsibility on the police services and local authorities to develop statutory partnerships to prevent crime and enhance community safety by means of Community Safety Orders. We recognise how plagued many neighbourhoods are by continual anti-social behaviour by individuals or groups of individuals.[42]

It seems certain that zero tolerance policing, as cited in the above examples, has had some kind of effect on crime rates, especially in the short term. However, there has been considerable resistance to the concept from senior police officers in other constabularies. To reiterate an earlier point, Charles Pollard has argued that its implementation may actually instigate further social problems.[43] Rather than 'nipping crime in the bud' we might see disorder on the scale of that which erupted in the inner-city riots of the 1980s and on some of the lonely and forgotten 'outer-city' or 'peripheral' estates in the 1990s UK.[44]

Research into zero tolerance-style policing is only just beginning and the long-term repercussions of these strategies remain to be seen. In the meantime there is likely to be much speculation, but if the view that 'what happens in the United States will happen in the UK' holds, then one possible development is that described by Jerome Miller of the National Centre of Institutions and Alternatives, and one identified by John Wadham in his contribution to this volume:

> There is a danger that zero tolerance can intensify the criminalisation of an entire class. The way things are going now, nearly 75 per cent of African-Americans and millions of Hispanics will have criminal records — having being booked and charged — by the time they reach 35. We have cities where one young black male in three is either in prison, on probation or awaiting trial.[45]

Clearly the situation in the UK is different, but there is the possibility that groups in underclass-type positions may be increasingly criminalised. Furthermore, this process may be perceived to be a result of deficiencies in the character of individuals. In doing this, the more complex processes underlying the creation of poverty and the economic rationality guiding the response of some people to this condition may be overlooked. The question which arises here is whether the police should be expected to tackle all of these problems.

Concluding points

This paper has examined one dimension of relatively recent debates about zero tolerance policing. It has attempted to consider the relationship between policing policy and practice and the political economic context in which this occurs.

Most police work is directed towards the excluded members of society, a group who are frequently labelled as an 'underclass'. The individuals belonging to this group change significantly over time and place, but it generally refers to socially isolated geographical areas with a high incidence of poverty and various other forms of social disadvantage. Due to a number of interrelated forms of structurally generated social exclusion and changing patterns of behaviour some groups have been involved in disorderly and criminal behaviour. The relationship between the underclass and the police service is complicated, especially in the case of zero tolerance.

For example, the diversity of notions of 'zero tolerance' poses a number of analytical problems, especially the lack of clarity with regard to its meaning. There are major variations between the UK and the USA. It would also appear that there are significant differences between different forces in the UK. It is noted elsewhere in this book that, in Cleveland, 'zero tolerance' has targeted known burglars in specific towns.[46] In the Metropolitan Police District, policing strategies have been designed to remove the disorderly from public places such as commercial districts and subways. This suggests that there are different rationales underpinning different 'zero tolerance' strategies.

More crucially, there is a lack of consensus within the tripartite structure of the police service with regard to the applicability of zero tolerance policing strategies in the UK. Despite its promotion by the Home Office and central government, key members of the Association of Chief Police Officers (ACPO) have expressed scepticism about its utility. Charles Pollard, for instance, has described it as a 'short-term fix and long-term liability'.[47]

The main concern is that insensitive policing of marginalised and excluded groups could lead to an escalation of conflict between the police and the policed, resulting in disorder on a much larger scale than has been seen for many years.

In terms of the history of policing zero tolerance, it is business as usual in two ways. First, it is consistent with the core functions devised in the early 19th century. Second, it tends to target the poorest members of society who are sometimes cast as an 'underclass'. Liberal criminologists and senior police officers alike claim that the police alone cannot tackle complex and deep-seated social problems, such as crime and poverty. Throughout the late 1980s and 1990s the government became tired of such excuses. Instead, they demanded that the service provides value for money, primarily in the form of measurable reductions in crime. Zero tolerance has won acceptance because it requires the police to demonstrate this by processing as many people through the criminal justice system as possible.

In the last analysis, the relative success or failure of zero tolerance awaits judgement. It would be a safe bet to say that it will have some impact and reduce the level of crime and disorder in particular geographical areas. However, it cannot respond adequately to the problems of social exclusion, poverty and the 'underclass'. This is significant because most policing targets the 'underclass'. Given that few politicians and senior police officers nowadays seriously dispute the link between crime and poverty, this does not augur well for the futures of policing and wider society.

Notes

1   Dr Chris Crowther, Lecturer in Criminology, Faculty of Applied Social Sciences and Humanities, Buckinghamshire University College.

2   See, for example, Pollard, C. (1997) Zero Tolerance: Short-Term Fix, Long-Term Liability. In Dennis, N. (ed.) *Zero Tolerance: Policing a Free Society*. London: Institute of Economic Affairs. Charles Pollard is Chief Constable of Thames Valley Constabulary.

3   Reiner, R. (1997) Policing and the Police. In Maguire, M., Morgan, R. and Reiner, R. (eds) *The Oxford Handbook of Criminology*. Oxford: Clarendon Press, p 726. The idea of an 'underclass' in general, and specifically in relation to policing, changes significantly over time and space. The extents to which it is gendered and racialised are particularly salient.

4   See Morgan, R. and Newburn, T. (1997) *The Future of Policing*. Oxford: Clarendon Press; Crowther, C. (1997) *The 'Underclass' Debate: the Police Policy Process and the Social Construction of Order*. Unpublished PhD Thesis: University of Sheffield.

5   For example:

> 'Zero tolerance' is all about sweeping clean those inner city junctions where tourists and professional commuters briefly encounter the dispossessed underclass — the mad and the sad, as well as the bad (Morgan, R. (1997) Swept Along by Zero Option. *The Guardian*, 22 January).

6   Cohen, P. (1979) Policing the Working Class City. In Fine, B., Kinsey, R., Lea, J., Picciotto, S. and Young, J. (eds) *Capitalism and the Rule of Law*. London: Hutchinson, pp 118-36; Jefferson, T. (1993) The Racism of Criminalisation: Policing and the Reproduction of the Criminal Other. In Gelsthorpe, L. (ed.) *Minority Groups in the Criminal Justice System*. Cambridge: Cambridge Institute of Criminology, pp 26-46. According to the rhetoric of UK Prime Minister, Tony Blair, 'zero tolerance' is primarily concerned with the 'workless' classes.

7   Walker, A. (1990) Blaming the Victims. In Murray, C. (ed.) *The Emerging British Underclass*. London: Institute of Economic Affairs Health and Welfare Unit, pp 49-58.

8   Dahrendorf, R. (1985) *Law and Order*. London: Stevens.

9   The continued intractability of these social problems has recently been identified by Oppenheim, C. and Harker, L. (1996) *Poverty: the Facts,* revised and updated 3rd edition, London: CPAG; Povey, D., Taylor, P. and Watson, L. (1996) *Notifiable Offences: England and Wales, July 1995 to June 1996*. Home Office Statistical Bulletin, 18/96. London: HMSO; and Mirlees-Black, C., Mayhew, P. and Percy, A. (1996) *The 1996 British Crime Survey, England and Wales*. Home Office Statistical Bulletin, 19/96. London: HMSO.

10 Murray, op cit; Murray, C. (1994) *Underclass: The Crisis Deepens*. London: Institute of Economic Affairs.

11 Westergaard, J. (1995) *Who Gets What? The Hardening of Class Inequality in the Late Twentieth Century*. Cambridge: Polity Press; Marshall, G., Roberts, S. and Burgoyne, C. (1996) Social Class and the Underclass in Britain and the USA. *British Journal of Sociology*. Vol. 47, No. 10, pp 22-44; and Levitas, R. (1996) The Concept of Social Exclusion and the New Durkheimian Hegemony. *Critical Social Policy*. Vol. 16, No. 1, pp 5-20.

12 See, for example, Jordan, B. (1996) *A Theory of Social Exclusion and Poverty*. Cambridge: Polity, pp 110-1.

13 Scarman, Lord (1981) *The Brixton Disorders 10-12 April 1981: Report of an Inquiry by the Rt Honourable the Lord Scarman OBE*. Cmnd. 8427. London: HMSO, p 4.11.

14 This is also well demonstrated in King, M. and Brearley, N. (1996) *Public Order Policing: Contemporary Perspectives on Strategy and Tactics*, Leicester: Perpetuity Press.

15 Newburn, T. and Morgan, R. (1994) A New Agenda for an Old Bill. *Policing*. Vol. 10, No. 3, p 144; Home Office (1993) *Police Reform: A Police Service for the Twenty-first Century*. Cm. 2281. London: HMSO; Police Foundation and Policy Studies Institute (1995) *Independent Committee of Inquiry Into the Roles and Responsibilities of the Police*. London: PSI.

16 See Pollard, op cit, p 129.

17 See Crowther, op cit.

18 John Alderson, the former Chief Constable of the Devon and Cornwall Constabulary, used this term when interviewed by the author. See ibid.

19 Police Foundation and Policy Studies Institute, op cit.

20 Home Office (1993) *Circular 114/84: Manpower, Effectiveness, Efficiency in the Police Service.* London: HMSO; Audit Commission (1990) *Effective Policing — Performance Review in Police Forces.* Audit Commission Police Papers, No. 8. London: HMSO.

21 Home Office (1993), op cit and Audit Commission (1993) *Helping With Enquiries: Tackling Crime Effectively.* Police Paper No. 12. London: HMSO.

22 These changes are enshrined in the Police and Magistrates' Courts Act 1994; Audit Commission (1994a) *Cheques and Balances: A Management Handbook on Police Planning and Financial Regulation.* Police Paper No. 3. London: HMSO; Audit Commission (1994b) *Cheques and Balances: A Framework for Increasing Police Accountability.* Police Paper No. 14. London: HMSO. For a review of some of these changes, see Leishman, F., Cope, S. and Starie, P. (1995) Reinventing and Restructuring: Towards a 'New Policing Order'. In Leishman, F., Loveday, B. and Savage, S. (eds) *Core Issues in Policing.* London: Longman; McLaughlin, E. and Murji, K. (1995) The End of Public Policing? Police Reform and the 'New Managerialism'. In Noaks, L., Levi, M. and Maguire, M. (eds) *Contemporary Issues in Criminology.* Cardiff: University of Wales Press.

23 Scarman, op cit.

24 Alderson, J. (1981) *Submission to Scarman: the Case for Community Policing.* London: HMSO. For an overview of the research into this style of policing, see Koch, B. and Bennett, T. (1993) *Community Policing in Canada and Britain*, Research Bulletin, No. 34, London: Home Office Research and Statistics Department. These authors argue that although there are few organisational structures in place to formalise community policing strategies, various philosophies of this style of policing have been incorporated into police thinking. See ACPO (1990) *Strategic Policy Document: Setting the Standards for Policing: Meeting Community Expectations.* Report of a Working Party. London: ACPO.

25 Scarman, op cit.

26 Section 106, Police and Criminal Evidence Act (PACE) 1984.

27 For a critique of the wisdom of this approach, see Reiner, R. (1995) Policing by Numbers: the Feel Good Fallacy. *Policing Today.* Vol. 1, No. 3, pp 22-4.

28 Crowther, op cit.

29 The Association of Chief Police Officers.

30 Hoddinott, J. (1994) Public Safety and Private Security. *Policing.* Vol. 10, No. 3, p 163.

31 Chaudhary, V. and Walker, M. (1996) The Petty Crime War. *The Guardian,* 21 November; Johnston, P. (1997) Mean Streets Where They Test the Zero Option. *The Daily Telegraph*, 8 January; Letts, Q. (1997) Joining the Resistance in the Big Apple. *The Times*, 24 January; and Read, S. (1997) Below Zero. *Police Review*, 17 January.

32 Chaudhary and Walker, op cit.

33 Metropolitan Police (1995) *Policing Plan 1995/96.* Scotland Yard: Metropolitan Police.

34 Cited in ibid.

35 Bratton, W.J. (1997) Crime is Down in New York City: Blame the Police. In Dennis (ed.), op cit; and Bratton, W.J. (1996) How We Cleared Up New York. *The Sunday Times,* 24 November.

36 For an overview of 'partnership policing' and other similar strategies, see Gilling, N. (1996) Policing, Crime Prevention and Partnerships. In Leishman, F., Loveday, B. and Savage, S. (eds), op cit.

37 Johnston, op cit.

38 Zero Tolerance: There Should be No Blind Eye to Crime. *The Times,* Leading Article, 19 November, 1996.

39 Chesshyre, R. (1997) Enough is Enough. *Telegraph Magazine*, 1 March, pp 20-26.

40 Orr, J. (1997) Strathclyde's Spotlight Initiative. In Dennis (ed.), op cit.

41 Ellis, W. (1996) Justice of the First Resort. *The Sunday Times*, 24 November.

42 Michael, A. (1997) *First Steps in Consultation on Crime and Disorder*. Home Office News Release, 149/97, 12 June.

43 Pollard, op cit, p 129.

44 Scarman, op cit; King and Brearley, op cit.

45 Miller, J., cited in Chaudharay and Walker, op cit.

46 Dennis, N. and Mallon, R. (1997) Confident Policing in Hartlepool. In Dennis (ed.), op cit, pp 68-70.

47 Pollard, op cit.

Chapter 7

Begging, Vagrancy and Disorder

Roger Hopkins Burke

Introduction

Begging and vagrancy have been a central focus of 'zero tolerance' policing strategies introduced both in the USA and the UK. This should come as no surprise, for, as was noted in my earlier chapter – 'A Contextualisation of Zero Tolerance Policing Strategies' – it is a policing philosophy theoretically informed by the 'broken windows' thesis,[1] which proposes that targeting and removing minor incivilities helps to eliminate factors that make a community appear more inviting to serious crime. Consequently, the targeting of beggars, vagrants and more anomalous categories such as unsolicited windscreen washers – 'squeegeemen' – was central to the policing revolution instigated by Mayor Giuliani and Police Commissioner William Bratton in New York City. In November 1996 the Metropolitan Police implemented 'Operation Zero Tolerance', in collaboration with the City of London Police and the British Transport Police, in King's Cross, London. The initial purpose of the strategy was to target and prevent crimes that were a particular problem in the locality, such as drug-related criminality and prostitution.[2] The emphasis was soon directed towards the targeting of particular groups such as beggars and the homeless.[3] Subsequently, such strategies have become very attractive to politicians – from both ends of the political spectrum – in the UK and have received widespread publicity in the media.[4] Beggars and vagrants are now widely perceived as a legitimate target for a vigorous police intervention.

This paper seeks to address a conundrum that raises significant issues for those charged with the responsibility for policing areas in which beggars and vagrants congregate. On the one hand, beggars and vagrants can provide an intimidating presence to be negotiated by ordinary people going about their legitimate activities; on the other hand, there is substantial evidence that they constitute an excluded group worthy of humanitarian consideration.

The structure of the paper is as follows. First, there is an examination of the concept of begging located in an historical context. Second, there is a consideration of the phenomenon of begging and vagrancy in contemporary society. Third, there is a discussion of a small empirical study of beggars conducted in the contemporary urban context that provides us with insights into the lives and motivations of people involved in begging and vagrancy. Finally, there is a consideration of the implications of these findings for future zero tolerance-style policing initiatives in the UK.

Begging in historical context

An examination of begging and vagrancy in an historical context in the UK enables us to reach the following three conclusions. First, begging has existed throughout history. Second, it has been most common at times of economic recession and social upheaval. Third, in terms of the conundrum outlined at the outset of this paper, the authorities have always tended to favour some form of 'zero tolerance intervention' on the grounds of protecting the status quo and/or social order in preference to a more humanitarian intervention. The following examples will serve to illustrate these propositions.

The 14th century response to begging and vagrancy – the *Statute of Labourers 1349* – prescribed the death penalty for any one who gave money to a beggar deemed fit to work. This legislation was instigated by landlords unable to find cheap labour in the aftermath of the Black Death and who took action to maintain the system of feudal obligations.[5] The 16th century response – the *Punishment of Rogues, Vagabonds and Sturdy Beggars Act 1597* – was passed at a time of mass unemployment caused by the demobilisation of thousands of military personnel and sought to regulate and control the apparent hordes of economically deprived men roaming the countryside.[6] This legislation allowed for the transportation of convicted beggars to the new colonies for use as manual workers and servants, and was widely seen as an effective way of dealing with a dangerous class of desperate men who posed a serious threat to public order.[7]

A further explosion in the number of beggars occurred as a consequence of the major socio-economic disruption that accompanied the great industrial revolution of the late 18th and early 19th centuries. Large numbers of people left the countryside to seek employment in the new industrial towns and cities. When work could not be found an unemployed population of hungry job seekers was created who turned to begging in order to survive.[8] This situation was exacerbated by the regular downturns in the trade cycle that occurred throughout the 19th century. For example, the recession between 1815 and 1820 combined with high bread prices resulted in large-scale unemployment and the creation of a mass of tramps who needed to beg to survive. A zero tolerance – rather than a humanitarian[9] – intervention remained the fundamental response to this problem throughout the period. In the depression year of 1869, for example, there were 17,541 prosecutions for begging, which compares with an average of 9,000 a year during the prosperous period between 1870 and 1875.[10]

There was a similar situation during the first half of the 20th century. For example, the Boer War (1899-1902) destabilised the economy and the job market to such an extent that there was a huge increase in begging and sleeping rough in London. Demobilisation following the First World War in 1918 produced mass unemployment and disabled war veterans,[11] while the inter-war years in the UK were characterised by the appeals of the war disabled, economic slump on an unprecedented scale, mass unemployment (2.8 million), the continuation of the *Poor Law Act*, the Board of Guardians and the dreaded 'means test': in a word, poverty. The official response to poverty, begging and vagrancy during this period can hardly be considered humanitarian.

It was in the years following the Second World War that there was a dramatic improvement in the situation. The post-war boom and full employment meant that few people needed to beg through economic necessity. The relatively few who were unfit for work were the beneficiaries of the new social security system, unemployment and sickness benefit, retirement pensions, and national assistance for those without national insurance contributions. The substantially reduced ranks of beggars now predominantly consisted of men with alcohol-related problems living in derelict buildings and sleeping rough.[12]

The return to begging on a large scale occurred following the collapse of the long post-war economic boom and the retreat from the welfare state that has epitomised the subsequent government response.[13] From 1973 onwards the growing world recession reintroduced mass unemployment to the UK, and increasingly tougher rules limiting welfare benefit to certain groups can be seen as a major reason why there are now greater numbers of beggars on the streets of London and other major cities in the UK.[14]

Begging in the contemporary UK

The traditional vagrant with alcohol-related problems continues to be strongly represented among those begging on the streets of the UK.[15] Many are mentally ill, and their presence on the streets is at least partially explained by care in the community policies.[16] The great majority of those forced onto the streets of the UK during the 1980s and 1990s have, however, been the unambiguous victims of the long economic recession that commenced in 1973 and the subsequent restructuring of the economy. Unable to find a job or having been made redundant, many have been overwhelmed by a sense of disillusionment:

> Many have parents who have been unemployed for ages and they have seen no chance of getting a job themselves so they come onto the streets. ... Once on the streets they face stark options ... begging is one.[17]

The significant defining characteristic of the vast majority of the new beggars to have emerged on the streets in the UK during this period has been their youth. Many are teenagers who have had to run away from home due to abuse, violence or the inability of parental income to support a child. These people make their way to the cities and become involved in a 'street culture' which involves sleeping in doorways, hanging out, looking rough and begging. Governmental policies have been cited as explanation for the existence of this street subculture.

Changes to social security entitlement in 1988 meant that 16 and 17-year-olds lost their automatic right to benefits and 18 to 24-year-olds saw a dramatic reduction in the amount of money they could claim. Caroline Adams from the charity 'Action for Children' estimated that this was a contributory reason why 75,000 16 to 17-year-olds had no source of income whatsoever.[18] Nick Hardwick, Director of Centre Point, responding to a speech by the then Prime Minister, John Major, who previously had been highly critical of beggars, commented:

> The reason young people beg is simple; they don't have any money. What does the Prime Minister expect them to do? Before 1988 surveys by Centrepoint found that none of them begged. Since benefits were changed for youngsters the numbers have risen steadily.[19]

Later in the year he added:

> Before 1988 you simply did not see young people begging and sleeping rough. ... We used to get about 700 young people a year into the private rented sector. The day after the changes were introduced it became impossible to get anyone a private rented place and the begging and sleeping rough began.[20]

The experiences of history have been repeated. Major economic and social upheaval has forced large numbers of people into poverty and homelessness and many of these have taken to begging on our streets. Furthermore, with the continuing experience of economic downturn, the official response increasingly moved away from any vestiges of humanitarianism. First, there were the changes to the welfare benefit system that provided the preconditions for people going onto the streets in order to beg. Second, there was the redefinition of these people as a social problem and increasing demands that something be done about them. It was a message that gained support from politicians at both ends of the political spectrum seeking populist support and it was in this context that 'zero tolerance' policing strategies targeting beggars were first introduced in the UK.

There is undoubtedly a widespread assumption among the public that the welfare state looks after the poor and inadequate. Consequently, those found begging on our streets can be considered shirkers and the workshy. These assumptions have been undoubtedly exacerbated by media stories that suggest that beggars are in some way 'bogus'. For example, the Reverend Ken Hewit was reported calling for the streets of South Kensington to be cleared of beggars, claiming that most are bogus:

> I have heard of beggars who collect £100 an hour. ... When you consider that it is tax free, it makes an income of around £50,000 a year.[21]

The concept of the bogus beggar is a semantically interesting one. It is interesting to speculate as to exactly what qualifications a person requires to be considered a bona fide beggar. There appears to be a general consensus that they should be penniless and preferably homeless. It is certainly criminal deception to falsely claim to be these things. For example, a man received a fine and a 12-month suspended prison sentence after it was discovered that he travelled in his 'L' registration Astra from his home in Hereford to Sheffield each day in order to beg.[22] Nevertheless, there appears to be no consensus definition of a legitimate beggar. For example, a London magistrate urged the public not to give money to beggars as she had just sentenced a Bosnian woman for begging with her 14-month-old daughter.[23] She appears to have failed some unwritten residency test.

In short, there are undoubtedly those who make false claims to their status, for example, those who proclaim that they are homeless when in reality they have accommodation. Nevertheless, there appears to be little evidence to suggest that begging is a particularly lucrative way of life, and indeed the literature suggests that virtually all beggars have one thing in common, their poverty, although this may well be a relative concept.[24] On the other hand, general public assumptions of the adequacy of the welfare state, compounded by media stories of dishonesty, provide an excellent context of public legitimation for the assertive, zero tolerance policing of beggars and vagrants.

It was in this socio-economic context that an empirical study of the pattern of begging in Leicester was conducted.

The Leicester study[25]

It was the purpose of the Leicester Study to investigate the lifestyles and motivations of people found to be begging in that city. It is the intention here to briefly reconsider data that informs the conundrum posed at the outset of this paper, for if, on the one hand, beggars and vagrants provide an often intimidatory presence to be negotiated by ordinary people, then their activities merit close police attention; if, on the other hand, they can be considered an excluded group unjustly treated by society, they are indeed worthy of humanitarian consideration.

Interviews were conducted by Philip O'Brien from the first week in May 1996 to the first week in June 1996. A total of 40 beggars were encountered at different times during that period and they were all invited for interview. None refused.[26]

All but two of the people encountered begging in Leicester were males and three-quarters of these were over 25 years of age. The great majority (80%) were long-term homeless and this was the case regardless of age. Younger people were more likely to be sleeping on the floors of their friends or living in squats, while older people were far more likely to be 'living rough'. Begging was a long-term and regular reality for the majority (62% had been begging for more than a year). Furthermore, those who had been begging the longest were far more likely to be sleeping rough (40% had been begging for more than a year and were sleeping rough).

It was possible to distinguish between two ideal types of beggars. Those with 'somewhere to go', whether it be their own home, a squat or a friend's flat, were far more likely to beg for a short period until they acquired sufficient funds to satisfy a specific need, for example, something to eat, while those who were sleeping rough were likely to focus virtually all the conscious part of their lives on begging. It is certainly the case that this latter group were far more likely to have alcohol-related problems than the former. However, both groups can be objectively classified as homeless.

The great majority (82.5%) said that they spent the money they had received from begging on food. A large minority (35%) admitted to spending their money on alcohol and these can clearly be identified as members of the hard-core group who had been sleeping rough long-term. Surprisingly, over half of the sample denied buying alcohol with their begging money, while less than a quarter admitted to using illegal drugs. Slightly over one half (57.5%) acknowledged receipt of state benefits. This is a rather low figure compared with other studies[27] and it may reflect a 'don't volunteer incriminating information to the authorities' mentality or simply a low take-up of entitlement.

Without doubt, the people encountered begging on the streets of Leicester were by any objective criteria seriously economically disadvantaged and worthy of sympathetic consideration. There is, however, a strong case for the regulation of their activities.

Most people in the study chose to go begging when and where they thought they were most likely to receive money. The most popular times were those, such as the rush hour and the lunch period, when more people were out and about, and the most popular places were those crowded city areas with narrow access where people were unable to easily avoid beggars. This undoubtedly involves some degree of tacit intimidation.

There is competition among beggars for the best 'pitches' and there appear to be self-regulating mechanisms by which these are 'allocated'. There is evidence that intra-group violence is an essential aspect of the vagrant way of life and it is extremely likely that physical coercion underpins much activity in the begging underworld.[28] The vast majority of beggars encountered also claimed to have been the victims of both verbal and physical abuse from members of the public. There is clearly a case for the regulation of the activities of beggars both in the interests of the general public and in order to offer some protection to those involved in this way of life.

The research evidence suggests that the police in Leicester have managed to maintain a reasonable balance between maintaining order and providing some protection to beggars. Less than a half of those interviewed during the course of the study had been warned by the police for begging on the street, while less than a third had been arrested for this offence. Nearly two-thirds had been arrested for offences other than begging, with the most common offence being 'assault' and 'drunk and disorderly'. The evidence of the Leicester Study suggests that the police are fairly tolerant of beggars, unless they are 'in breach of the peace' and behaving in an aggressive fashion. Some of those interviewed suggested that some police officers actually 'look out' for the safety of the more vulnerable beggars. These findings might help to explain the generally positive attitude of beggars towards the police in Leicester.

We will now consider these findings in a wider context.

Discussion and conclusion

It was noted at the outset of this paper that begging and vagrancy have been a central focus of zero tolerance policing strategies both in the USA and the UK. Furthermore, it was observed that these activities are now widely perceived – by the public, politicians from both ends of the political spectrum, and the media – as a legitimate target for a vigorous police intervention. Indeed, the lessons of history show that at times of major economic and social upheaval the authorities have always tended to favour some form of zero tolerance intervention in order to maintain social order.

Evidence suggests that beggars can be considered in the main an economically excluded group. There are inevitably those who falsely represent their circumstances but there is little evidence to support the suggestion that begging is an economically rewarding way of life. Beggars are essentially members of a class of people (underclass or workless class) who are *excluded* from the normal basic standards of living most of us would consider acceptable – they can be simply characterised as an *excluded* class.

In terms of one part of the conundrum introduced at the outset of the paper, the message appears unambiguously clear: people begging on our streets have legitimate rights and are worthy of humanitarian consideration. On the other hand, there is some evidence that large numbers of beggars and vagrants can provide a disconcerting and sometimes intimidating presence to be negotiated by ordinary people going about their legitimate activities in the business areas and shopping centres of our cities and towns. These are the venues in which members of the excluded social classes come into contact with members of the included social classes (those of us with the good fortune to have access to jobs and/or opportunities). Members of the former group can appear frightening to some of the latter – particularly when beggars have a self-conscious awareness of their own intimidatory presence. The Leicester Study uncovered no evidence of *overt* 'aggressive begging'; nevertheless, intimidation takes on more subtle forms. Many of those interviewed admitted to seeking out those areas of town with the highest congregations of relatively affluent people – choosing those specific places where geographical space is narrowly constrained and members of included society are forced into the close proximity of the excluded. They were undoubtedly aware of the intimidatory nature of these actions.

It would be relatively easy for the police to take a particularly assertive stance with a group of people who tend to have few friends, supporters or champions. It would be relatively easy to simply clear our main business precincts of beggars and vagrants – to introduce a policy of zero tolerance. Furthermore, it is extremely unlikely that this disparate group would be the focus of even loosely organised social unrest. In many ways they would make an easy target for a police service seeking the support of the wider community and certainly for politicians seeking the popular vote.

The real problem is this: what would we do next? It is doubtful that a further criminalisation of these people would provide a cost-effective and long-term solution to their problems. Warnings and cautions might divert some people on the fringes of begging and vagrancy from these activities, but it is extremely likely that the great majority – particularly the large group with identified alcohol-related problems – would simply be diverted to other geographical locations with a lesser police presence or perhaps diverted into the commission of criminal acts.

Such a strategy would be selective in favour of commercial interests and would be suggestive of the Los Angeles-style policing approach described by Mike Davis where modern technological surveillance, private security and public sector policing conspire to protect affluent and business areas by excluding the dispossessed from their precincts.[29] It is a selective policing strategy that targets and criminalises the deprived and disadvantaged, the sad and mad, in order to protect business and commercial interests. It is simply *unfair*.

People have a right to be protected against aggression, intimidation and incivilities, and it is appropriate that the police take action to ensure this protection. The zero tolerance-style targeting of beggars is nonetheless fraught with dangers and there are three closely linked reasons why this is so. First, there is the pragmatic case. The criminalisation of begging and vagrancy will not provide a cost-effective and long-term solution to the problems of poverty and inequality in our society. In short, the incarceration of large sections of society would be an extremely expensive and short-term way in which to maintain social order. Second, there is the normative case. Targeting and criminalising the deprived and disadvantaged is simply *unfair*. The nature of power relations in our society means that policies tend to be directed at those who are already socially excluded and marginalised. Third, there is the threat to civil liberties. Without appropriate safeguards, there is a real danger of a slow drift to a society intolerant to those who fail to conform to a narrow definition of normality. It is that conundrum that this paper has sought to address: the need to regulate and control begging and vagrancy while heeding the rights and liberties of disadvantaged citizens.

Possible solutions to that conundrum will be needed at two distinct but closely interconnected levels of intervention. First, at a micro-(or street) level, action against beggars and vagrants will only be successful in the long term if the police act in partnership with other agencies – both professional and voluntary – in dealing with all aspects of the problem. There seems absolutely no point in introducing zero tolerance policing strategies that simply remove beggars from the streets and displace their activities to other areas or that criminalise and incarcerate them at great expense to the taxpayer. Furthermore, a micro-strategy will only work if there is a political commitment to deal with the long-established societal problem of economic exclusion. Hence, at a macro-(or societal) level there needs to be a policy commitment to ensure the reintegration of excluded groups back into the mainstream of included society.

Notes

1   Wilson, J.Q. and Kelling, G.L. (1982) Broken Windows. *Atlantic Monthly*, March, pp 29-38.

2   Metropolitan Police (1995) *Policing Plan 1995/96*. Scotland Yard: Metropolitan Police.

3   See Crowther, C. (1998) 'Policing The Excluded Society' in this volume.

4   There have been frequent references to beggars from politicians in the past few years and these have been reported widely in the press. For example, the then Prime Minister John Major said

in a speech in Bristol in May 1994:

> ... Beggars are offensive and could drive shoppers away from cities. The law should be used vigorously to deal with them. .... It is not acceptable to be out on the street. ... There is no justification for it these days. The problem is as old as the hills. It is a very offensive problem to many people who see it. In areas that depend on tourism, it is very damaging to everybody if that sort of activity continues. If people are in desperately straitened circumstances we have a social security net *(The Guardian*, 28 May 1994, p 1).

Recent political discourse on begging and vagrancy can be clearly located in the context of debates on 'zero tolerance' policing. Michael Howard was the first government minister to refer to the issue, but his Labour Party successor, Jack Straw, visited New York in the summer of 1996 to observe zero tolerance policing in action and returned impressed with what he had seen. See Travis, R. (1996) Atlantic Cuffings. *The Guardian*, 21 November. In the long run-up to the 1997 General Election his party leader, Tony Blair, backed police action against beggars in an interview published in the January edition of *the Big Issue*: Interview with Tony Blair. *The Big Issue*, 8 January 1997.

5   Postan, M. (1972) *The Medieval Economy and Society.* Harmondsworth: Penguin.

6   Coldham, P. (1992) *Emigrants in Chains.* Maryland: Genealogical Publishing.

7   See Slack, P. (1974) Vagrants and Vagrancy in England, 1598-1664. *Economic History Review.* Vol. 27, pp 360-79; Beier, A.L. (1985) *Masterless Men: the Vagrancy Problem in England 1560-1640.* London: Methuen.

8   Rogers, N. (1991) Policing the Poor in Eighteenth-Century London: The Vagrancy Laws and their Administration. *Histoire Sociale - Social History.* Vol. 24, pp 127-47.

9   The 'humanitarian' response was institutionalised in the infamous Poor Law Amendment Act 1834. This Poor Law created a system of poor relief based on 'less eligibility'- that none receiving relief should be better off than the lowest-paid labourer - and also a system of deterrence - that the conditions of accepting relief, particularly entry into the workhouse, would be so shaming as to deter people from applying for it and push them instead into the labour market. Williams, F. (1989) *Social Policy: A Critical Introduction.* Oxford: Polity Press.

10 Ibid.

11 Ibid.

12 See Conroy, J. (1975) *Some Men of Our Time: A Study of Vagrancy.* MA Dissertation, Department of Sociology, University of Leicester; Archard, P. (1979) *Vagrancy, Alcoholism and Social Control.* London: Macmillan. Their lives are brilliantly illustrated in the autobiography of reformed alcoholic/ vagrant turned chess grand master John Healey, who portrays the terrifying world of the vagrant alcoholic and beggar, the 'grass arena' where the law is enforced with the broken bottle, the boot and the knife. Healey, J. (1988) *The Grass Arena.* London: Faber and Faber.

13 See Jessop, B. (1990) *Regulation Theory and the Transition to Post-Fordism.* Oxford: Polity.

14 Rose, L. (1988) *Rogues and Vagabonds.* London: Routledge.

15 They often coalesce into informal groups of beggars trying to pool their money for alcohol. Studies suggest that they are usually male and middle-aged. They have lost touch with their families, their marriage has broken down or else they have never been married. Most are un-skilled, having spent time labouring in the construction industry or in the armed forces. See, for example, ibid; Healey, op cit; Conroy, op cit; Archard, op cit.

16 Murdoch, A. (1994) *We Are Human Too: A Study of People Who Beg.* London: Crisis. The programme based on the closure of psychiatric hospitals and an attempt to reintegrate patients back into the community was flawed from the outset by a lack of resources. Former patients have often been denied the support which would enable them to successfully manage their own homes. The result of this situation has been large numbers of mentally ill people slipping into a twilight world of cheap bed and breakfast hotels or latter-day doss houses and forced out onto the streets to beg. See Conway, J. and Kemp, P. (1985) *Bed and Breakfast: Slum Housing of the Eighties.* London: SHAC.

17 *The Guardian,* 2 December 1992, p 16.

18 *The Guardian,* 11 June 1994, p 34.

19 *The Guardian,* 28 May 1994, p 1.

20 *The Guardian,* 14 December 1994, p 29.

21 *The Guardian,* 17 July 1993, p 4.

22 *The Times,* 17 February 1994, p 5.

23 *The Times,* 29 May 1993, p 5.

24 See Conroy, op cit; Archard, op cit; Healey, op cit; Rose, op cit; Rogers, op cit; Murdoch, op cit.

25 There have been a number of studies of begging and vagrancy in London at various points in history. This is not surprising as London has always been a focus for those seeking their fortune and has traditionally ended up as a dumping-ground for tramps, vagrants, alcoholics and others who have failed. See Orwell, G. (1974, originally 1931) *Down and Out in London and Paris.* Harmondsworth: Penguin; O'Connor, P. (1963) *Britain in the 60s: Vagrancy.* London: Methuen; Working Party on Vagrancy and Street Offences (1974) *Working Party on Vagrancy and Street Offences Working Paper.* London: HMSO; Archard, op cit; Rose, op cit; Rogers, op cit. Leices-ter, on the other hand, is a medium-size provincial city without the attractions of the capital.

26 See Hopkins Burke, R. and O'Brien, P. (1998, forthcoming) *Begging in Leicester: A Prelimi-nary Study.* Scarman Centre for the Study of Public Order Occasional Paper Series. Leicester: University of Leicester.

27 For example, 80% of people found begging in a study in London were found to be in receipt of state benefits. See Murdoch, op cit.

28 Ibid. Further research could seek to examine possible hierarchical stratification within the so-cial world of begging and how this is internally policed.

29 Davis, M. (1990) *The City of Quartz: Evacuating the Future in Los Angeles.* London: Verso.

Criticism: Short term, expensive

Chapter 8

The 'Slide to Ashes': An Antidote to Zero Tolerance

Bob Knights[1]

Introduction

This paper proposes that 'zero tolerance'-style policing is based on an inappropriate reading of the 'broken windows' thesis[2] and presents an alternative model which it is argued provides a more accurate reflection of that philosophy. It is proposed that successful crime prevention strategies should be sustainable, long-term and cost-effective, whereas certain applications of zero tolerance are labour-intensive and/or short-term, for example, the high-profile police operations instigated in the King's Cross area of Central London in November 1996.[3] The widespread publicity granted to that experiment makes little mention of the ongoing costs involved in maintaining the Special Unit responsible for implementing that strategy. The so-called zero tolerance policing strategy instigated by William Bratton in New York City involved the recruitment of a further 7,000 police officers.[4] Zero tolerance-style strategies are invariably short-term and expensive.

A model is introduced – the 'slide to ashes' – devised as a means of predicting and preventing crime and disorder in educational premises, but, it is proposed, with wider potential applications in society, that has close similarities with the 'broken windows' thesis. The model can be used to identify and predict a sequence of events increasing in seriousness and impact; it identifies the relevance of minor incidents and the need for swift reparative action.[5] It is similar to zero tolerance-style approaches in that it advocates that the smallest of transgressions against set standards needs a quick and firm response; discipline, in the broadest of interpretations, needs to be maintained, and offenders dealt with appropriately. It is suggested, however, that the more subliminal ethos of the 'slide to ashes' is more sustainable, cost-effective and more easily adopted and incorporated into management practices than the short-term solution of zero tolerance-style policing. Furthermore, while the 'broken windows' thesis asks questions about cause and seeks remedies, and the 'slide to ashes' can identify and predict, 'zero tolerance' deals with little more than the outcomes of earlier problems.

The 'slide to ashes'

The 'slide to ashes' is best described as a sequence of events that leads from an almost insignificant act to the total destruction of a school by fire. There are nine component stages, and while they are presented in order of contributive relevance, there might be a slight variation in the order, depending on site specificity. Essentially this is of little consequence as the whole is far greater than any single component.

1. Litter

The sequence starts with the appearance of litter. In a normally clean site this is the warning that action needs to be taken immediately. In a situation where litter has been allowed to accumulate, the 'slide' has already started. There is a parallel here with the 'broken windows' thesis, which asserts that the first signs of disorderly behaviour need to be checked in order to prevent its spread and development into more serious crime.

There are three distinct aspects to the arrival and establishment of litter within a school. First, it gives the impression of dirt and disorder, it is an incivility and can be seen as symptomatic of a lack of positive action from within. The perpetrators are allowed freedom to continue to set a lower standard for the premises and signal their own lack of care or concern. Second, to an outsider, at least two messages are given: (i) that the general standard of acceptable conduct is now lower than previously, and (ii) if the acceptance level of allowing litter is such, then the possibility of a lower degree of security and safety within the school is greater. Third, rubbish and waste are a component part of the initial fire-set. Litter can be a target of a zero tolerance-style strategy and therefore a similarity exists between the two approaches. The difference is in the manner of responding to the problem: a word of advice, or a strict enforcement of the Litter Act 1958.

2. Graffiti

The second component of the 'slide to ashes' is graffiti. Isolating several features that collectively could be considered vandalism is deliberate. Graffiti, litter, damage and wear and tear could all fit under the umbrella. Each is defined separately, however, because it is felt that exposure to each element makes the 'slide' more identifiable.

Vandalism is not defined in criminal law as an offence. It is a useful generic term, which at best is convenient, and at worst distortive. Any strategy must be based upon analysis and research of accurate data. Placing an assortment of different acts under one umbrella completely loses focus and meaning. The term is, therefore, not used: graffiti is a specific act, a minor break-in is a burglary, and a deliberate fire is arson. It is imperative that all are not only recorded separately but also in a manner that allows proper analysis.

Consider two school premises. The former is litter and graffiti free. It need not sparkle in the sunlight but it looks stable, cared for and clean. The latter is visualised with litter and rubbish in and around the premises. This may lead to the possible next step, which will be the advent of graffiti. If litter is not cleared away, why should graffiti be cleaned off? The graffitist can enjoy the display of the 'tag' and the kudos of their peers. The longer it remains, the more permanent; the more permanent - the more strongly the 'norm' is established. The grounds have litter being blown about and the walls and doors have become home for graffiti. Cues are beginning to emerge that may be favourable to further crime. Skogan indicates how we should deal with the problem of litter and graffiti:

> I asked the owners of a bar in West Philadelphia how they kept their place so clean. They showed me. Inside the bar is a bucket of paint and brushes. As soon as the kids mark the outside, they come out with the paint and paint it over right away. That is the only way.[6]

At this point the 'slide to ashes' is in its early stages and, in relative terms, easier to arrest. Attitudes and management are the first and cheapest tools.

Litter and graffiti were two of the issues tackled by Strathclyde Constabulary's Spotlight Campaign.[7] Focusing on those areas that the public felt had taken second place to major crime, every available officer was tasked towards the same, particular topic. This was not called 'zero tolerance' but 'community policing with the gloves off'. Again, the argument within the 'slide' is that prevention is better than costly cure.

3. Fair wear and tear
The next stage in the 'slide to ashes' is easy to describe generally but difficult to define precisely or specifically. Having seen the advent of litter and an invitation to graffiti, the next part is a differentiation. It is suggested that fair wear and tear and minor criminal damage are two distinct and separate entities. The former is the result of genuine use and accidental damage, both of which will always happen, while the latter is deliberate and intentional. This is a further justification for avoiding the bland category of 'vandalism', which is considered too wide and all-consuming. The essential point is to make repairs promptly[8] on the grounds that damage often invites further attack and causes considerable inconvenience to users.[9]

4. Minor criminal damage
The next stage is the transition from fair wear and tear into minor criminal damage.[10] Those premises that have either prevented or reduced the incidence of the former will offer less favourable cues to offending than the site where there is visible evidence of decay. Those schools which abrogate responsibility for controlling this decline will encourage more criminal damage.[11]

The 'slide to ashes' is now taking a more discernible form and direction. Litter has encouraged graffiti, fair wear and tear has probably become enmeshed with deliberate minor criminal damage – although they should be kept as separate analytical categories – and the premises is following the sort of progression suggested by the 'broken windows' thesis. The overall hypothesis was that general incivilities and antisocial behaviour are indicative of crime and disorder. This leads to the community (read school) abrogating responsibility for control, and thus more criminal damage results:

> Vandalism [*their word*] can occur anywhere once communal barriers – the sense of mutual regard and the obligation of civility – are lowered by actions that seem to signal no-one cares.[12]

5. Unauthorised use

The next stage of the 'slide' is for the grounds to be used for unauthorised purposes. Educational establishments have long suffered from a slight identity crisis – if they are private places, why are they open to local children? If they are public places, why cannot the grounds be used out of hours? Certainly, personal instances are known where local children are encouraged to unofficially use the grounds in return for information about outsiders with criminal or antisocial intent. This community interaction can be very beneficial.[13]

The point to consider is whether the appearance and management approach has resulted in a smart, clean, ordered environment in which intruders will be conspicuous and obvious, or an area that resembles an unloved climbing frame, open to all. The demarcation between the two is very important.

The pessimistic picture that may now be emerging is of the littered, abused building and grounds, used by whoever pleases, for whatever purpose. A word concerning quantification is needed in respect of the extent of these components. The rubbish does not need to be knee-deep, there is no need for a second window to be smashed, or for gangs to be roaming the grounds. The process is gradual and the quantities may be small, and this is possibly a very important point. As the evidence may appear inconsequential it can easily be dismissed or ignored. There is a need to record small details,[14] and it is suggested that as a jigsaw needs all the pieces, so all the evidence is required to make considered decisions on recognising and addressing the component parts.

6. Minor burglary

Previous research emphasises the significance of the first minor burglary.[15] This not only increases the probability of further break-ins but also provides the preconditions for arson:

> As far as our sample is concerned, there seems to be a strong relationship between victimisation through arson and victimisation through damage and burglary. ... Schools which have been suffering from damage or from burglary should think seriously about their precautions against arson.[16]

> Schools are also more likely to be set on fire (which may be a consequence of burglary) than all other classes of property.[17]

> A school which has suffered one or more break-ins may become a target for an arson attack.[18]

> Arson is often associated with a burglary and accounts for a much greater financial loss than would be expected for burglary alone.[19]

7. Minor fire

The link between minor burglaries and minor fires has been illustrated above. As can now be seen, small fires are significant and they need to be reported and dealt with. Responsibility for ensuring that this is done should be shared by staff, pupils, governors, parents and the local community. Without such intervention the next component will become evident in the form of repeated burglaries.

8. Major or repetitive burglary

The accumulation of the components of the 'slide to ashes' has now resulted in the premises being open to random, unchecked attacks and misuse. Research into school burglaries in a particular area of Manchester emphasised the significance of responding adequately to the first burglary:

> From an unrealistically optimistic viewpoint, if all repeat victimisations in a year could be prevented, this would account for nine in ten crimes, leaving 33 rather than 296.[20]

This viewpoint is shared by other researchers.[21] Furthermore, others have noted that larger schools with less supervision and more open spaces are at greater risk.[22]

9. Major fire

There is one final section left to the 'slide', and that is the 'ashes'. It is suggested that if the previous sequence of events is allowed to run its course, it will be contributing to a major fire. It has been stated that not every component is a prerequisite, that areas can interchange, and it is acknowledged that there will always be the exception. As a holistic concept, however, there is much support to be found in the case studies that follow.

Methodology

Three case studies were undertaken in order to establish the efficacy of the 'slide to ashes'. Two of the studies are longitudinal,[23] and these were chosen as the sites had both suffered total devastation by arson and new schools had been built in their place. In these cases interest is focused on how the predictions and prevention came too late, and how that situation has been redressed, or not, in the new schools. The third study is cross-sectional[24] and was selected because of the positive and overt philosophy towards antisocial behaviour in and around the school.

The case studies

Case study no. 1

The school in question, a small Junior Mixed Infant, sits on the periphery of an old mill town on the edge of the Pennines in north-west England. After an escalating history of crime and arson attacks, the building was eventually razed to the ground in 1983. Significantly,

> The blaze came as the climax of a series of attacks at [the School]. There had already been several small fires. Break-ins took place virtually every weekend.[25]

The site was visited in June 1990 and the head teacher and staff interviewed regarding the history and circumstances surrounding the loss of the old school and the circumstances of the new building. The staff were resolute in their commitment to the pupils, who in turn were generally very well behaved; the obvious problem was the manner in which the local community viewed the school.

This may be a good example of one of the fundamental problems of zero tolerance-style approaches: that is, there is seldom concern over the link between the commission of a crime and the cause. Had the school been subjected to some form of zero tolerance policing, probably everyone in or around the premises would have been stopped, searched and questioned. The law of averages would dictate that an arrest for something would follow, the problem would fade, and attention would be switched elsewhere. Unfortunately, at that stage the problem returns and in the long term little is gained.

Lono long term strategy.

The problem here, in essence, is that nearly two sides of the school are surrounded by open green fields, a wonderful environment but with a potential for trouble. The situation was exacerbated by the fact that the remaining two sides were bordered by public housing stock that at the time had a particularly high void rate. The net result was that the site had no formal or informal social control, no surveillance and no sense of belonging. There were simply insufficient people with any interest in the place to exert care or control. Tellingly,

> locals could not be relied upon to raise the alarm if something went wrong. (Nobody is known to have rung the Fire Brigade when St Oswald's went up in flames!).[26]

At the time of this first visit the school had been in use for three years and already there were signs of decay evident. Windows had been sprayed and attempts to clean the polycarbonate sheeting had worsened the damage. Light fittings had been smashed, burglaries attempted and the guttering and pipework on the outside store removed. The current craze was to put a scaffold plank across from the roof of the store to the school roof and to use the roof sheeting as a slide. Ironically, this roof material had been chosen because of the high 'slip factor', which was seen as a deterrent feature. There was also a collection of debris on the roof ranging from housebricks to 'no parking' cones consistent with 'unrepaired damage'. This suggested that an immediate repair and clean philosophy was not in practice. A year previously it was reported:

> the worst thing that has happened to date is that a few stones have been lobbed onto the roof.[27]

The fact that over a year later this debris had increased to include housebricks and parking cones should have signalled a clear message.

A further visit took place in June 1996. The building itself had continued to be vandalised. Several windows had been broken, an interesting development as the original glazing was polycarbonate sheeting and usually very resilient. What does need to be considered, however, is that the determination to commit the attack and achieve damage had increased in proportion to the protection. This would surely signify a reduction in concern about possible retribution, no formal surveillance, no intervention from the neighbours, no attempt to manage litter and damage, and no community ownership.

Similar problems were identified with a new detached nursery building completed in 1994 on the same site. During the summer of 1995 the wooden fencing surrounding the building was broken down. A repair was attempted but that was also broken. A decision was then made to make no further repairs. In the short term there was a cost saving but the long-term outcome was more damage.[28] Lights surrounding the buildings have been broken and criminal damage inflicted. These remain unrepaired. Attempted burglaries continue.

During the period 1987 to 1990 certain discernible signs had appeared and had generally not been dealt with. From the visit it appears that over the period 1990 to 1996 matters had deteriorated. It is suggested that at present the most powerful preventative factors for this building are the manner and matter of its construction, but the first part of the 'slide to ashes' appears very evident. A comment from the previous head teacher may seem painfully prophetic: 'I think we all knew in the early eighties it was only a matter of time'. History, hopefully, will not repeat itself here.

Case study no. 2
This school is set in an area of Liverpool that at the time of the first visit in June 1990 was acknowledged as being a 'rough, tough' neighbourhood, a description encapsulated by observations of the local Police Crime Prevention Officer:

> If your photographer goes over the road by himself either him or his cameras won't be coming back.[29]

The original school had suffered crime and arson and had finally been burned to the ground in 1984. The staff and pupils followed a nomadic existence as described here by the head teacher:

> These three years of camping out in another school were horrendous. We were just refugees.[30]

The school was located in the centre of an area of dense public housing stock and although it has playing fields on two sides it directly adjoins housing where the pupils live. Not only is the community immediate, but they were involved in discussions about the new school: that very important link was established and maintained. The outcome was that the building was not anonymous and unloved, but a very real part of the area. Again, an example of the permanency and social responsibility suggested as being so essential for sustained efficiency.

The management ethos of the school was clear and positive. The education of the children was paramount and an orderly environment would be provided to achieve that objective. The wider issue of the community was also acknowledged and they had been involved in the replanning of the school. When the premises were opened, they received a visit from John Butcher, the then Junior Education Minister, who emphasised the community link:

> You can talk about all the hardware under the sun, but the other half is the community caring for its environment. It is their school; theirs to look after and value.[31]

Around the grounds there was not a scrap of litter or rubbish. Internally, floors were clear, equipment out of sight and everything very tidy. When these issues were raised, much of the credit was given to the caretaker – a very committed woman with apparently limitless energy. There was a healthy participative culture among the staff and the emphasis was on the provision of a learning environment for the pupils:

> It was important that the children felt comfortable inside the school. Once they went in through the street doors we wanted them to forget about the danger and the poverty of the surrounding area and to put them at ease.[32]

The school was revisited in June 1996. The grounds had benefited from some planting with shrubs and small trees. The interior had been redecorated, but after six years that is understandable. The caretaker had retired and had been replaced by a 'site manager' fulfilling the same functions. In essence, the situation was exactly the same as previously. There was one exception: an attempt had been made to force one of the shutters over a ground floor window. The signal that needs to be heeded is that a part of the 'slide' has re-emerged and must be monitored very carefully. The words of the original caretaker have added significance in light of this event:

> I used to get called out three or four times a week, sometimes more. Kids were breaking into the school and vandalising all the time.[33]

One attempt in seven years is a very good record when neighbouring schools are reportedly still suffering from crime and arson.

Case study no. 3
Located in an area of North London, the school is a split-site secondary serving an area that includes both high-density public and private housing stock. The intake is multicultural and represents a varied cross-section of society. The Lower School is tucked away in an enclosed site, several hundred metres from the Upper School. Traditional materials were used in its construction and an interesting angular design was incorporated for the two-storey premises. An extension is at present under construction. Funding is by the Local Education Authority.

The catalyst for action at the school emerged during 1991 when there were behavioural problems and a prolonged occurrence of minor criminal damage in the girls' toilets on both sites. This had been preceded by an increasing amount of litter and sporadic outbreaks of graffiti, and a pervasiveness of general incivilities. The deputy head made it quite clear to the school that this was unacceptable and that the money being spent on repairs was not being used for more beneficial items for the pupils. In effect, this established the parameters for the acceptable behaviour expected. Soon after a School Coun-

Slide to ashes better
BUT not used correctly: used correctly in STA

cil, despite some opposition, and later a School Action Group were formed.
course classic themes of the 'broken windows' philosophy and of the 'slide

A competition was held to design a logo and a 'Clampdown' Action Group Committee to which pupils are elected was formed. There is a constitution that details exactly the responsibilities of the members, a Premises Sub committee, a 'Speakeasy' – a pupil-based counselling service, a shop in the Lower School, and a Fund-Raising Sub committee. [Each member is required to sign an agreement in respect of their conduct and responsibilities as both an elected member and a pupil of the school.]

It is not contended that this is an isolated example of where pupils and staff work together, but what is of interest is the management approach, and the specific points of reference within the operation of 'Clampdown' and the School Council. An obvious parallel must be drawn with McGregor's Theory Y as detailed in Hickson and Pugh:

> People will exercise self-direction and self-control in the arena of objectives to which they are committed.[34]

From the evidence to date, this shared ownership approach has succeeded. The pupil members have regular structured meetings with staff, are involved in Induction Days, speak to new parents and act in the best interests, as perceived, of both pupils and staff. A possibly more interesting aspect of the ethos is, however, the setting of specific targets within the Premises Sub committee portfolio. Within the brief are:

> ... an anti-graffiti campaign; policing the vandalism budget; bringing to the attention of Clampdown members any student known to be vandalising the school property; keeping the student body up to date regarding money used for replacing items through vandalism; promoting an anti-litter campaign in both buildings.[35]

There have been tangible results from these practices that reflect the 'slide to ashes' within a very short space of time. Criminal damage stopped; a budget was agreed whereby the savings on repair were spent on mutually agreed items; the Lower School was declared a litter-free zone and a recycling scheme undertaken. [This internally prioritised and generated approach, it is contended, reflects the cost effectiveness and sustainability that would not be evident through the harsher zero tolerance ethos.] *harshness not effective*

What has resulted from this management approach is that the first three key components of the 'slide to ashes', that is, litter, graffiti and criminal damage have been targeted as 'non-starters'. They were recognised as unacceptable and the potential forerunner to a more extensive problem, and a concentrated campaign [focused on prevention.] Weekly graphs are even produced to ensure standards are kept. The deputy head freely admitted that it has not been an easy task and requires constant servicing, but, to date, in five years the approach has been vindicated by the absence of crime and arson, and an agreement that the components of the 'slide to ashes' should not emerge.

This approach has attracted much praise and the school is extensively involved with *Crime Concern*,[36] conferences, environmental projects, Youth Action Groups, Youth Achievement Certificates, *Victim Support*[37] and Education/Industry Partnerships. This shared management philosophy overtly puts a responsibility on the pupils to ensure the safety and security of their own school.

The arguments previously presented in terms of treating the cause of the problem and not just the outcome, of sustainability, of cost effectiveness, of management, and of achieving results in an acceptable manner, are all represented in this case study. The positive and sought-after results have indicated the identification, shared ownership, problem-solving approach that is offered as the preferred option to zero tolerance.

Conclusions

This paper has sought to present a crime prediction, intervention and prevention model in the form of the 'slide to ashes'. It is a sequential development that, it is proposed, identifies the small and inconsequential, and charts their development into a more serious set of outcomes. There is a similarity with the 'broken windows' philosophy – that provides the theoretical foundations for zero tolerance-style policing strategies – and other literature that endorses the need to: (i) acknowledge the potential growth of minor incidents, and (ii) seek immediate and appropriate intervention techniques to prevent escalation.

Approaches of this kind are almost by definition both longer-term and multi-disciplined, and are in contrast to the more overt zero tolerance-style policing strategies that have been discussed. The main contention has been that the former are more cost-effective; more easily integrated into management and practice, and, therefore, more sustainable; and involve a wider set of actors. There is a stronger requirement for more participation from more groups, an act that in itself promotes shared responsibility and ownership.

This may be contrary to the zero tolerance policing approach that could follow a simplified rational choice model of motivated offender, suitable target or ones conducive to offending and lack of capable guardian. Remove one, and the triangle collapses and no crime results. A very true scenario, but one that does not really consider the cause or attempt to treat it. It is proposed that both the 'slide to ashes' and parallel research can offer more in terms of prediction, treatment and sustainability.

While there is serious, violent crime in society, there will probably always be a need for firm, fast, reactive policing, commensurate to the offence and the offender. What has been presented here is a case for the more subliminal, shared and socially acceptable approach to long-term crime prevention. An approach that draws together more of the participants that make up society and the community itself. The words of Rod Morgan and Tim Newburn give a haunting prediction:

> The main reason zero tolerance is on the agenda and likely to remain there, is that the phrase has enormous resonance. The attractiveness of the notion is its apparent simplicity. The danger is that it easily becomes simplistic.[38]

It is hoped that before these words are proven, the alternative approaches are given as much opportunity and exposure in order to prove their worth.

Notes

1   Bob Knights, MBE, MSc, is Area Crime Prevention Co-ordinator with the Metropolitan Police and Chair of the Association of Chief Police Officers Technical Committee.

2   Wilson, J.Q. and Kelling, G.L. (1982) Broken Windows. *Atlantic Monthly*. March, 1982, pp 29-38. See the 'Editor's Introduction' and 'A Contextualisation of Zero Tolerance Policing Strategies' in this volume for a full discussion of these positions.

3   Ellis, W. (1996) Justice of the First Resort. *The Sunday Times,* 24 November.

4   Bratton, W.J. (1997) Crime is Down in New York City: Blame the Police. In Dennis, N. (ed.) *Zero Tolerance: Policing a Free Society*. London: Institute for Economic Affairs.

5   See Burquest, R., Farrell, G. and Pease, K. (1992) Lessons from Schools. *Policing.* No. 8 (Summer), pp 148-55. This produced a report on repeat victimisation of school property in an area of Manchester. Bridgeman (1996) *Crime Risk Management: Making it Work*, London: HMSO, discusses risk management in schools and the need for a holistic approach to include community involvement. Also the Fire Prevention Association (1992) *Prevention and Control of Arson in School Buildings*. London: FPA. The FPA state that the majority of fires are arson.

6   Skogan, W. G.(1990) *Disorder and Decline: Crime and the Spiral Decay in American Neighbourhoods*. New York: The Free Press, p 39.

7   Strathclyde. *Police Review*, 4th April 1997, p 18.

8   This observation is endorsed by several writers. See Skogan, W.G. (1981) *Coping with Crime: Individual and Neighbourhood Reactions*. London: Sage; Wilson, S. (1979) Observations On the Nature of Vandalism. In Skyes, J. (ed.) *Designing against Vandalism*. London: Design Council; White, D. (1979) Vandalism and Theft in Schools: How Local Authorities Can Defend Themselves. In ibid.

9   See Riley, D. (1980) An Evaluation of a Campaign to Reduce Vandalism. In Clarke, R.G. and Mayhew, P. (eds) *Designing Out Crime*. London: HMSO.

10   Criminal Damage is an offence under the Criminal Damage Act 1971.

11   Knights, R. (1995a) *Making the Streets Safe with the UK Crime Prevention Police*. Japan Urban Security Research Institute Supplement No. 6. Tokyo: JUSRI.

12   Wilson and Kelling, op cit, p 38.

13   See ibid, p 39; Gill, M. and Hearnshaw, S. (1997) *Personal Safety and Violence in Schools*. Sudbury: DofEE Publications.

14 See Bridgeman, op cit.

15 Hope, T. (1982) Burglary in Schools. In Hope, T. (ed.) *Implementing Crime Prevention Measures*. London: HMSO.

16 Burrows, J., Leitner, M., Shapland, J. and Wiles, P. (1993) *Arson in Schools: Report to the Arson Prevention Bureau*. Arson Update 1/93. London: Arson Prevention Bureau, pp 32-33.

17 Hope, op cit, p 11.

18 Burrows et al, op cit, p 3.

19 The Fire Prevention Association, op cit, p 5.

20 Burquest et al, op cit, p 152.

21 Farrell, G. and Pease, K. (1993) *Once Bitten, Twice Bitten: Repeat Victimisation and its Implications for Crime Prevention*. Crime Prevention Unit Paper No 46. London: Home Office; Pease, K. (1997) Crime Prevention. In Maguire, M., Morgan, R. and Reiner, R. (eds) *The Oxford Handbook of Criminology*. Oxford: Clarendon Press.

22 FPA, op cit; Felson, M. (1994) *Crime and Everyday Life*. Thousand Oaks, CA: Pine Forge Press; Gill and Hearnshaw, op cit.

23 By studying the same groups at different points in time, longitudinal surveys seek to provide a stronger basis for providing explanations. Such explanations are usually in terms of relating individuals' behaviours to initial characteristics of those features of those same individuals, to maturational features or to intervening events. This is facilitated by collecting data from the same individuals at different, and often key points in their lifespan. Jupp, V. (1989) *Methods of Criminological Research*. London: Routledge, p 42.

24 With cross-sectional designs a sample of individuals is selected and interviewed at a particular point in time about their present attitudes or behaviours and, in some studies, about what has happened in the past. There is, then, the capacity to collect both past and present data, perhaps to find relationships within and between these, but with cross-sectional designs the validity of past data is inevitably dependent upon the memories of respondents. Ibid, p 39.

25 Surkes, S. (1989) Far From a Fortress but Designed to Last for Keeps. *Times Educational Supplement*, 24th February, p 17.

26 Ibid.

27 Ibid.

28 Knights, R. (1995b) *Making Safe Streets: Making Safe Houses*. Japan Urban Security Research Institute Supplement No. 5. Tokyo: JUSRI.

29 Personal communication with the author.

30 Shreenan, M. (1989) *Security Gazette*, May, p14.

31 Hadfield, G. (1989) School Becomes Fortress to Fight Arson Attack. *Sunday Times*, 5th March.

32 McLellan, A. (1989) Case Studies - School Security. *Building,* April, pp 62-7.

33 Hadfield, op cit.

34 Hickson, D.J. and Pugh, D.S. (1989) *Writers on Organisations*. Middlesex: Penguin, p 159.

35 Salisbury School (1991) *Premises Sub-Committee Portfolio*. London: Salisbury School, p 3.

36 The charity *Crime Concern* was established in 1989. It was 'pump-primed' with government money and thereafter encouraged to seek sponsorship, particularly from the commercial world, to support its crime prevention projects and training programmes for practitioners. Morgan, R. and Newburn, T. (1997) *The Future of the Police*. Oxford: Clarendon Press.

37 *Victim Support* (formerly the National Association of Victim Support Schemes, NAVSS) provides services to victims at a local level. It works from the assumption that many crime victims are likely to be traumatised by their experience and that support from friends, family, or neighbours may be insufficient or simply unavailable. Zedner, L. (1997) Victims. In Maguire et al (eds), op cit.

38 Morgan, R. and Newburn, T. (1997) Tomorrow's World. In *Policing Today*, June.

Chapter 9

Concluding Remarks

Roger Hopkins Burke

This volume has provided a forum for informed debate between academics and practitioners with a range of professional interests and viewpoints on the issue of zero tolerance policing. It has been the purpose – in the spirit of the allegedly new post-ideological political times – to consider the differences and commonalities of a range of perspectives with a view to seeking an agreed basis for the adoption of this style of policing.

It was argued in chapter two – 'A Contextualisation of Zero Tolerance Policing Strategies' – that the general concept of proactive, confident, assertive policing has universal validity. On the other hand, it was proposed that the specific strategies implemented within the parameters of that general theoretical context need to be sensitive to the consumer demands of different communities and must be considered 'fair' by the various interest groups that constitute those micro-societies.

Chapter three – 'A Question of Confidence: Zero Tolerance and Problem-Oriented Policing' – outlined and discussed recent policing initiatives introduced by the Cleveland Constabulary and proposed that 'zero tolerance' and 'problem-oriented policing' are both part of the long established community-based tradition in the UK and are hence compatible philosophies. It was proposed that the short-term zero tolerance strategies have allowed officers to reclaim the streets and implement the longer-term strategies of problem-oriented policing, crime prevention and community safety.

Significantly, these initiatives were introduced in response to widespread public demand. Consequently, there continues to be considerable local public support and there has apparently been no serious social disorder. Cleveland is a predominantly white working-class area which has lost much of its traditional employment with the radical restructuring of the UK economy that has occurred during the past 20 years – there are very few members of ethnic minorities – and the deviant and criminal minority have roots from within this traditional community.[1] It is a community that can be considered to have a high level of mechanical solidarity[2] with a relatively shared social consensus. The police are not perceived as an external force making war against the local community but as the professional representatives of that community, targeting 'a particular minority, criminals'.[3]

The police service faces more complex problems in areas containing diverse and fragmented interest groups. It is in such cases – particularly where there have been high concentrations of members of ethnic minority groups[4] – that accusations of discrimination have been made against the police.[5] Chapter four – 'Zero Tolerance Policing: Striking the Balance, Rights and Liberties' – discussed the civil liberties implications of zero tolerance-style policing. We were warned that scarce police resources might be allocated to trivial issues such as street offences to the exclusion of more serious forms of crime, with a parallel discriminatory targeting of the poor and, in particular, young black men. We are asked to consider who is making these policing decisions and in whose interests they are being made.

These are important civil liberties issues which need to be addressed. Significantly, we are advised that the general public would prefer to see resources allocated for more serious cases rather than diverted to dealing with incivilities. This is a contentious argument. The public consider burglary and, for that matter, street robbery as important crimes worthy of priority intervention, but both these offences have been the target of zero tolerance-style intervention in the UK. Initiatives against street offences and incivilities, on the other hand, appear to have been extremely popular among the general public in both the USA and the UK and seem to have been introduced in response to vociferous public demand.[6] Street incivilities engender a serious fear of crime among the general public and there is considerable evidence that the public want something done about the problem.[7]

These observations should nonetheless sensitise us to the serious issue of political accountability. It has been argued most persuasively that the very disadvantaged groups highlighted as being the likely targets of discriminatory policing strategies are those effectively disenfranchised by a political system that, in reality – both in the USA and the UK – vies for the support of only two-thirds of the electorate.[8] There is a real danger that contemporary representative politics will – while successfully tuning in to the post-ideological collective 'mood of the people' – fail to address the concerns of the one-third of the population excluded from that new social consensus.[9] Organisations like Liberty are undoubtedly essential to protect and promote the interests of these excluded groups.[10]

Chapter five – 'Below Zero Tolerance: The New York Experience' – considered these civil liberties issues in the aftermath of the so-called 'zero tolerance' policing initiative in New York City.[11] The view that this style of policing is counter to the concept of policing by consent was disputed, and it was argued that when successful it is more in harmony with community wishes than the alternative widespread abandonment of public spaces to the perpetrators of incivilities. It was observed that many of the so-called 'underclass' and members of ethnic minorities have themselves been the victims of crime and have welcomed the declining crime rate and the simultaneous economic revitalisation of their communities. The more successful zero tolerance-style initiatives have been those that have consulted with the community before implementation and have heeded their concerns.

The notion that zero tolerance-style strategies leave the police with no discretion was rejected. There is a selective rather than a perpetual enforcement of all quality of life offences and this is part of an overall strategy – often incorporating other agencies – to target specific problems. We are told that zero tolerance-style policing is ultimately about refusing to accept that the public police service cannot seriously impact upon crime. Termed 'smarter policing', we are warned that it requires intelligence and flexibility to implement and that it is a far more difficult approach than the previously dominant highly bureaucratic, reactive, defeatist and, ultimately, remarkably unsuccessful model of policing that prevailed in the USA.[12]

Chapter six – 'Policing The Excluded Society' – considers the relationship between police policy and practice in the political context of the UK. We are advised that following the social unrest that occurred in the inner cities during the 1980s the preservation of public tranquillity became the top policing priority. More recently there has been a policy reversal and the prevention and detection of crime has taken precedence.

This shift took place in the context of rapid social, economic, political and ideological change. The Conservative Government came to reject the notion that the modern police service is primarily a peace-keeping organisation at the same time as they introduced reforms based on the disciplines of the market that required police performance to be measured in terms of the crime clear-up rate. It is notable, therefore, that zero tolerance-style policing strategies have focused on easily quantifiable incivilities and low-level disorder as part of an attempt to reduce crime.

It was the central contention of this contribution that the bulk of police work has throughout history targeted excluded groups in society. It is admitted that members of this 'underclass' are currently involved in disorderly and criminal activity, but we are told that this can be explained by a number of interrelated structural and behavioural factors. The crucial factor appears to be poverty.

The policing of excluded groups experiencing apparent poverty is the subject of chapter seven – 'Begging, Vagrancy and Disorder' – where it is recognised that there have always been beggars on our streets but that their numbers apparently increase significantly at times of rapid social and economic change. It is therefore proposed that they can be considered a legitimate *excluded* class worthy of humanitarian consideration. On the other hand, large numbers of beggars and vagrants provide an often intimidating presence to be negotiated by ordinary people going about their legitimate activities. Consequently, there is a good case for the rigorous policing of begging and vagrancy.

Undoubtedly, such policing initiatives would be widely popular with large sections of the public and, furthermore, it is extremely unlikely that this disparate group would be the focus of even loosely organised social unrest. They seem a relatively easy option for a public relations obsessed police service and politicians seeking office. In reality, there is of course no such thing as an easy option in the world of policing, and the paper presented three arguments as to why it is important to heed the rights and liberties of disadvantaged citizens while controlling begging and vagrancy.

Chapter eight – 'The 'Slide to Ashes': An Antidote to Zero Tolerance' – poses the possibility that there might be wider and more appropriate applications for 'broken windows'[13]-based 'nipping it in the bud' strategies than the assertive zero tolerance-style policing strategies that have been introduced in some constituencies. A model for intervening in schools identified at being at various stages of risk from vandalism is introduced and it is proposed that a timely intervention can reverse a process of decline. A more measured and non-confrontational community approach to dealing with problems than that offered by more assertive forms of policing is advocated. It is the main contention that the former are more cost-effective, sustainable and in keeping with a shared responsibility and ownership approach, more compatible, in a general community policing sense, with the approach advocated in the Scarman Report in the UK.[14]

We should note that the Scarman Report still provides the benchmark for the policing of a tolerant liberal society. A police service that wishes to introduce a proactive, assertive, confident policing strategy that has both widespread legitimacy and popularity with the general public needs to heed the lessons of Scarman and have the *consent*, *trust* and *participation* of the community. If there is a failure to heed that lesson, the initiative will be likely to end in failure, widespread dissent and disorder. It is potentially a style of policing that will enable the contemporary service to establish its own distinctive and central role in leading the challenge against crime and incivilities while at the same time leaving it highly dependent on the goodwill, support and widespread legitimation of the particular community it purports to serve.

Essentially, such policing strategies can only be successful in the long term if the police service pays heed to the civil rights and liberties of that community. The contemporary service should be about intervention and arbitration in the disputes and conflicts that inevitably impinge on our enjoyment of a lively and forward-looking organic and multicultural society. Such an approach requires tact, professionalism and consultation with *all* sectors of the community. The potential outcomes for a police service pursuing that approach include widespread acceptance, legitimacy, respect and the support of the general public. The service should not be used as a blunt instrument to help restore the repressive world of a monocultural mechanical solidarity. In short, proactive, confident, assertive policing strategies must be located in the context of a contemporary conceptualisation of community policing.[15]

Finally, it should be noted that positive, assertive policing does not have to lead to a massive and irreversible increase in the number of people incarcerated by the criminal justice process. Critics of zero tolerance-style policing strategies point to the extremely large percentage of the population – and an even larger percentage of black people – incarcerated in the USA.[16] This is a process that was already at an extremely advanced stage in that society long before the advent of the new policing revolution. Proponents have argued that the numbers in prison will decline as the long-term effects of that revolution filter through into society.[17] We will have to wait and see. Nevertheless, confident assertive policing does not have to lead to inevitable arrest. Many miscreants will get the message that the 'goalposts' of acceptable behaviour have been moved and a professional police service acting in a 'fair' fashion will find that they have considerable community support for these initiatives. Inevitably, there will be those who do not get the message. They will need to be dealt with *fairly* by the criminal justice process.

In short, there should be no return to the military-style policing strategies pursued by metropolitan forces in inner-city neighbourhoods in the UK during the late 1970s and early 1980s.[18] The case for zero tolerance-style policing lies clearly in the context of contemporary community crime prevention strategies.

Notes

1   Dennis, N. and Mallon, R. (1997) Confident Policing in Hartlepool. In Dennis, N. (ed.) *Zero Tolerance: Policing a Free Society*. London: Institute for Economic Affairs.

2   See Durkheim, E. (1964, originally 1893) *The Division of Labour in Society*. New York and London: Free Press/Macmillan.

3   Superintendent Ray Mallon speaking at the Conference on 'Zero Tolerance Policing' held by the Institute for Economic Affairs, Inter-Continental Hotel, Hyde Park Corner, London, 12 June, 1997.

4   See Durkheim, op cit.

5   See, for example, Lea, J. and Young, J. (1984) *What is to be Done about Law and Order?* Harmondsworth: Penguin; Wilson, J.Q. (1975) *Thinking About Crime*. New York: Basic Books.

6   See Terry Romeanes, 'A Question of Confidence - Zero Tolerance and Problem-Oriented Policing' in this volume. Kelling, G.L. and Coles, C.M. (1996) *Fixing Broken Windows: Restoring Order and Reducing Crime in Our Communities*, New York: The Free Press, provide a comprehensive account of the widespread support that such policing strategies have in the USA.

7   Kelling and Coles, op cit, cite myriad evidence of this fact.

8   See Galbraith, J.K. (1992) *The Culture of Contentment*. London: Penguin.

9   There are numerous examples from both sides of the Atlantic of politically motivated abuses of police operations. See Lea and Young, op cit, pp 234-7; Jefferson, T. and Grimshaw, R. (1984) *Controlling the Constable*. London: Muller, pp 36-45.

10 The American Civil Liberties Union (ACLU) has been a key agency in the resistance to legislation seeking to restrict the activities of beggars and vagrants in various parts of the USA. See Kelling and Coles, op cit, for a comprehensive account.

11 See, for example, ibid; Bratton, W.J. (1997) Crime is Down in New York City: Blame the Police. In Dennis, N. (ed.), op cit.

12 See in particular the account by the former New York Police Commissioner William Bratton in ibid.

13 Wilson, J.Q. and Kelling, G.L. (1982) Broken Windows. *Atlantic Monthly*, March, 1982, pp 29-38; Kelling and Coles, op cit.

14 Scarman, Lord (1981) *The Brixton Disorders 10-12 April 1981: Report of an Inquiry by the Rt*

Hon. the Lord Scarman, OBE. London: HMSO.

15 See Friedmann, R.R. (1992) *Community Policing: Comparative Perspectives and Prospects*. London: Harvester Wheatsheaf.

16 See Morgan, R. and Newburn, T. (1997) *The Future of Policing*. Oxford: Clarendon Press.

17 See Kelling and Coles, op cit; Bratton, op cit.

18 Lea and Young, op cit.

Index

Violence 22, 25, 26, 50, 63, 83

Crime at Work: studies in security & crime prevention
Volume One

Topics covered include:

robbery, commercial burglary, ram raiding, shoplifting, insurance fraud, violence against staff, crime on industrial estates, cheating in hotel bars, terrorism and the retail sector, the effectiveness of electronic article surveillance, customer and staff perceptions of closed circuit television, security implementation in a computer environment, and the advantages of in-house to contract security staff.

Edited by
Martin Gill

This ground breaking book contains a wealth of information which is of essential reading for all those interested in crime prevention, security, the motivation of different types of offenders, and the effectiveness of various security measures. Each article covers the theme of crime prevention. Papers incorporate the views of offenders, victims, customers and staff.

Crime at Work:
studies in security
& crime prevention

Until now there has been very little consideration of the extent, impact and patterns of crimes that occur in the work place. This important text suggests that such an omission is no longer justified. Produced in collaboration with business, the book reflects the growing realisation that effective responses to crime are based on the need to collect and share information.

"This book breaks new ground in many areas and contains a wealth of interesting facts and hard information."
Commercial Crime International

£25.00
ISBN 1 899287 01 9
240 pages
(index included)

1994

"A ground breaking piece of work because it draws on the experience of criminals and former criminals to show security experts...how to prevent crime."
The Independent

Crime at Work: increasing the risk for offenders
Volume Two

Topics covered include:

staff dishonesty, shop theft, violence in the work place, robbery, crime against business, fraud, shoplifting, drugs in pubs and clubs, the impact of data corruption on loss prevention practices, contract security staff, farm crime, product positioning and its vulnerability to theft, product counterfeiting, retail crime

**Edited by
Martin Gill**

This exciting new book in the 'Crime at Work' series builds on the success of Volume One. It focuses on crime risk management and provides exciting new case studies which examine the scale and patterns of crime and the impact that it has on different businesses. It suggests ways in which organisations can improve security, target resources, and evaluate offences.

**Crime at Work:
increasing the risk
for offenders**

This book contains a wealth of information which is of essential reading for all those involved with crime prevention, crime risk management and evaluating the effectiveness of various security measures.

£25.00
ISBN 1 899287 51 5
240 pages
(index included)

September 1998

Crime and Security: managing the risk to safe shopping

This significant text will be of interest to shop owners, retailers and managers, as well as those with special responsibilities for policing, private security, town centre planning and commercial development.

Adrian Beck and Andrew Willis

This important book offers unique insights into crime and its prevention in retailing. It compares and contrasts the priority given to security by town-centre and shopping centre managers, and it examines the use and effectiveness of current security measures.

Particular attention is paid to the role of private security guards and the 'privatisation' of policing in the retail sector. There is also a detailed examination of the use of CCTV, which is contrasted with the lack of information about its effectiveness.

Crime and Security: managing the risk to safe shopping

The study constitutes the only comparative analysis of crime and nuisance in town centres and shopping centres and, more importantly, it reviews the implications for crime control strategies in both environments - in the interests of both the retailers and shopping public.

"...excellent, readable material, containing useful, practical information that is of use to Crime Prevention Officers, Shopping Centre Managers and to students of retail crime policies."
Professional Security

£22.50
ISBN 1 899287 04 3
270 pages
(index included)

1995

This book is *"likely to become a standard reference for students of retail crime and security policies... (it) provides a stimulating introduction to a whole range of important issues, but is particularly significant for the research agenda it lays out."*
Professor Joshua Bamfield,
Centre for Retail Research

Learning from Disasters: a management approach
Second Edition

Topics covered include:

learning from hindsight, organisational reaction, safety culture, managing risk, learning from disasters, systems failures, lessons learned from fires, training, public enquiries, chance and disasters, information and disasters

Brian Toft and Simon Reynolds

This highly commended book demonstrates how a pro-active management approach provides a cost effective way to protect organisations both against human and financial losses.

This invaluable book is essential reading for all those involved in risk management, disaster planning and security and safety management. It is based on thorough research and is extremely practical and easy to read.

Learning from Disasters: a management approach Second Edition

It offers an important insight into the way organisations implement policies, systems and procedures to prevent future disasters from occurring. The message is very clear; where organisations fail to learn from disasters, history is likely to repeat itself.

Learning from Disasters is a tremendously important and invaluable text, with a strong message that cannot be ignored

£25.00
ISBN 1 899287 05 1
144 pages
(index included)

"...a relentless analysis of the way that things go wrong"
The Times Educational Supplement

1997

"An absolute must for the bookshelf"
Professional Security

"This book is commended to all those involved in disaster planning, implementation and testing"
Health and Safety at Work

Public Order Policing:
contemporary perspectives on strategy & tactics

Crime and Security Shorter Studies Series: No. 2

Topics covered include:

theories of crowds, police policy and training practices, developments in strategy and tactics, the policing of political, industrial, festival and urban public order events, the future of policing in a 'post-modern' society.

Mike King and Nigel Brearley

This highly commended book highlights the major 'watersheds' in the policing of political, industrial, festival and urban disorders and contains a wealth of material from interviews with senior police officers. The book is written in a clear and concise style, incorporating an extremely informative glossary of terms. This work is essential reading for both police practitioners and those studying or interested in the area of contemporary policing.

Public Order Policing: contemporary perspectives on strategy and tactics

"Mike King and Nigel Brearley are to be congratulated on this well documented and compelling analysis of the changing face of British public order policing. This timely and refreshingly accessible book ought to be essential reading for anyone seeking to understand the recent evolution of police crowd control methods, or eager to predict the future direction of police public order strategy and tactics."

Dr David Waddington
Sheffield Hallam University.

£14.95
ISBN 1 899287 03 5
128 pages
(index included)

1996

Issues in Maritime Crime: mayhem at sea

Crime and Security Shorter Studies Series: No. 1

Topics covered include:

fraud, piracy, arson, theft, deception, smuggling and drug trafficking. There is also a focus on containerisation, boat watch, insurance, registration and marking schemes, physical security measures and their potential to prevent offending.

Edited by Martin Gill

This path finding book offers new insights into aspects of maritime crime and its prevention. Its coverage of both domestic and international issues will appeal to all those interested in crime prevention, security and maritime issues.

Articles have been written by internationally recognised experts on maritime crime. This includes the police, HM Customs and Excise, a private investigator, as well as independent specialists and academic researchers.

Issues in Maritime Crime: mayhem at sea

Papers refer to real cases offering a fascinating insight into the threat posed by crimes that occur at sea. The information in this text suggests that internationally and domestically the official response to maritime crime has too often been unimaginative, misdirected and partial and has sometimes worked against the interests of crime prevention.

£12.95
ISBN 1 899287 02 7
80 pages
(index included)

"Any owner who is realistic enough to appreciate that crime is not merely something that happens to other people, would be well advised to study these papers."
Practical Boat Owner

1995

International Journal of Risk, Security and Crime Prevention

Topics covered include:

computer security, evaluating the effectiveness of CCTV, consequential loss, security shutters, arson, insurance fraud, regulation of the security industry, personal safety at work, the role of private investigators, security and crime prevention at home, protecting organisations from risk, racism, armed robbery, managing risk, violence at work, deviant drivers, crimes against business, security by design, commercial burglary, crime and loss control training, product contamination, repeat offences, household property crimes.

**Edited by
Adrian Beck
and
Martin Gill**

This exciting journal is at the forefront in examining and developing new policies in risk, security and crime prevention. It is the leading journal in its field and is fast becoming the essential reference point for risk and safety practitioners, researchers and policy makers across the world.

This dynamic journal aims to bridge the gap between theory and practice, providing a unique forum for the exchange of knowledge and expertise. The quality of content, presentation and advisory support is designed to distinguish it from all other journals in its field, making it the definitive journal for today's risk and security industry.

**Annual Subscription
Rate (1998):
£130.00 (£145.00
Overseas)**

a "resounding success"
Criminal Justice Europe

"It has clear potential for becoming essential reading on a truly international basis for all those with a responsibility for risk analysis, crime prevention and effective corporate and individual security"
Sir Peter Imbert

**Single issues £40.00
(£45.00 Overseas)
ISSN 1359-1886
280x210mm**

The journal is of a "high standard, informative, interesting and offering a fresh insight"
Kluwer's Handbook of Security

Crime, Order and Policing:
An International Journal

Topics covered include:

Crime Trends, National and International Policing Issues, Victimisation, Drugs and Crime, Crowd Behaviour, Civil Disorder, Zero Tolerance Policing, Researching Crime, Fear of Crime, Policing Measures and Initiatives, Crime Investigation Technologies, Explanations of Crime, Evaluating Crime Prevention Techniques, Criminal Justice Process, International Perspectives on Crime Control, Distortion and the Media, Moral Panic, Crime Statistics, Crime and the Media, Racial Harassment

Edited by Professor Rob Mawby

This distinctive new journal is at the forefront in addressing the issues of crime, order and policing within society. It facilitates debate on the problems which confront people, communities and societies and provides ideas and initiatives to tackle them.

The journal offers a unique forum for the exchange of information and expertise between academics and practitioners, bridging the gap between theory and practice.

1999 Annual Subscription Rate (1999): £97.00 (£112.00 Overseas) £55.00 (individual subscribers)

Crime, Order and Policing: An International Journal is essential reading for practitioners, policy makers and academics involved in the field of policing, community safety, local government, probation and prison services and all aspects of criminal justice, social science research, law firms, prisons, private and corporate security.

ISSN 1460-3780 Quarterly

The journal will include research based papers, case studies and informative review articles focused on key issues. it will address crime problems at local, national and international levels.

Regular features include:
- Up to the minute critiques of new developments
- 'A letter from...' Summarising recent developments in different countries
- 'Surfing the Crime Net' (a review of new material from the Internet)
- Book Reviews by Dr Anthea Hucklesby

Risk Management:
An International Journal

Topics covered include:

The Identification of Risk, Risk Management, Contingency Planning, Risk Forecasting, Recovery Programmes, Crises and Disaster Planning, Accidents, Environmental Threats, Human Error and Vulnerability, Insurance, Training and Education, Organisational Strategy, Models of Risk, Risk Perception, Risk Containment, The Role of the Media, Markets and Competition, Mathematical Analysis, Technological Citizenship, Ethical and Legal Aspects, Practical Information, Safety and Security, Human Behaviour, Expert and Professional Judgement, Public Relations, Customer Care, Financial Risk, Risk Policies, Risk Communication, Risk Assessments, Political Risk

Edited by Martina McGuinness and Martin Gill

Risk Management: An International Journal aims to facilitate the exchange of information and expertise across countries and across disciplines. Its purpose is to generate ideas and promote good practice for those involved in the business of managing risk.

All too often assessments of risk are crudely made and the consequences of getting things wrong can be serious, including loss of opportunities, loss of business, loss of reputation and even life.

1999 Annual Subscription Rate (1999): £160.00 (£175.00 Overseas)

Risk Management is essential reading for all those involved in managing risk. The journal will include research-based papers and case studies, literature reviews and ideas aimed at developing theory and practice. Papers are written by policy makers, professionals, researchers and academics, all leading experts in the field of risk.

ISSN 1460-3799 Quarterly

The editors of the journal are from the internationally renowned Scarman Centre at Leicester University. In addition the journal is supported by a prestigious advisory board which includes eminent practitioners and academics.